HAMLET, PRUFROCK AND LANGUAGE

ZULFIKAR GHOSE

First published 1978 by
THE MACMILLAN PRESS LTD
London and Basingstoke
Associated companies in Delhi
Dublin Hong Kong Johannesburg Lagos
Melbourne New York Singapore Tokyo

Printed in Great Britain by offset lithography by
Billing & Sons Ltd, Guildford, London and Worcester

British Library Cataloguing in Publication Data

Ghose, Zulfikar
    Hamlet, Prufrock and language
    1. English Literature – 20th century – History
    and criticism   2. Shakespeare, William.   Hamlet
    I. Title
    820'.9'00912   PR471

ISBN 0-333-23997-0

QUEEN: O Hamlet, speak no more.

Hamlet, III, iv, 89

. . . what I am, where I am, whether I am words among words, or silence in the midst of silence . . .

SAMUEL BECKETT: *The Unnamable*

Hamlet, Prufrock and Language

There is the world, here is my body which I believe has an existence, and these are words: words with which from time to time I wonder about my existence and try to puzzle out what relation it has with that world. I'm given to ecstasies, those moments of seeming comprehension when words no longer are words but are nevertheless there, in my mind, whirling as a pure essence and not as separable sounds which refer to objects, not merely complete sentences, but an entire language, its abstraction, all its meaning that's suddenly comprehended without the actual use of words, a music within the skull. It's as when I open the little bottle of rose-water to pour three or four drops of the precious essence into the dessert which I'm preparing to infuse into it a fragrance that belongs more poignantly and at the same time more elusively to the very idea of *the rose* than anything that could be distilled from roses; but later, a guest, lifting the first spoonful of grated carrots, boiled in creamy milk and thick with pulverised almonds and experiencing a vague aroma of roses, finds that he can neither distinguish the ingredients which appear only as ethereal sensations nor know from where the distant memory of roses is touching off perfumed currents in the brain, but yet is convinced that a knowledge of subtle meanings is dancing within the mind and in that moment of the sweet ecstasy when there is a conviction of understanding but no words to puzzle over, the mind and the rose are one.

That world and this body. There are times, of course, when I do not want to know, and the body, lying in the grass or sitting on a rock, prefers the chameleon's facility for self-dissolution; there is a contraction inwards, no desire to know anything, but suddenly, when the body is immersed in the blue ocean, say, there, in the water, there is a shimmering of the soul; and there are times when one envies the drop of dew its doomed brilliance. That drop of dew which Sylvia Plath's Ariel would become –

> And I
> Am the arrow,
>
> The dew that flies
> Suicidal, at one with the drive
> Into the red
>
> Eye, the cauldron of morning.

That dew to which Hamlet's flesh would melt, thaw and resolve itself. They take us to the ocean, plunging us into depths, these thoughts in which the self belabours definitions: water, most massive of abstractions; flowing but solid; the busy rivers and the ever-swelling ocean; John Berryman dives into the Mississippi and Hart Crane drops himself into the Caribbean; Virginia Woolf and Ophelia, too, in rivers of reality and of fiction; and Theodore Roethke in whose last poems the words are recreating the physical world in an obsession for metaphysical comprehension, cried towards the end, 'water's my will'. To say nothing of Prufrock who came to 'the chambers of the sea' and heard the mermaids singing. In enchantments, and then in refinements, of language, there's madness. Seeking an immersion in something other than the self, burdened by overwhelming questions, we drown ourselves in words. And, of course, the ecstasy leaves me when I emerge from the ocean and the sand sticks between my toes, the illusion of comprehension goes when the man frying fish on a fire of driftwood calls to his children playing on the beach, proving the banal utility of words, that former delicious abstraction quite lost, that beautiful, intoxicating ache in one's limbs induced by the water only a memory. The music was illusory, even the sea-shell you pick up releases no whisper from its hollow chamber, and you throw it back, a dead object. Life goes on, people eating deep-fried fish, repeating clichés about the weather, pointing to clouds which, they insist, resemble seals or sea-lions or whales.

What despair, then, again to be in the naked day, the blinding sunlight scooping the day's heat from the sand-dunes, and being compelled to change the angle of the parasol; what rage in the mind, then, whose convictions must remain transient, no more than the sudden stunning touch of a cold current in the warm Gulf waters, that ecstasy of *language* gone, replaced by the struggle to find the next word to say something. Visions turn to vapour; the dog, bounding down the beach, halts, contracts his body and defecates on the sterile sand. One doesn't have to be a prince to be overcome by a weariness of spirit.

From the beginning of *Hamlet*, there is a cry for answers to mysteries. Francisco in the second line of the play:

Nay, answer me. Stand and unfold yourself.

And Marcellus in the same scene:

Good now, sit down, and tell me he that knows, . . .

The demand for explanation: give us a meaning to these strange phenomena: tell us what these things purport: you are a scholar, Horatio, surely you with all your knowledge can explain?

'That can I,' says Horatio with the confidence of one who has no doubt that his learning has equipped him for answers to what is inexplicable to lesser minds, but presently he himself is exhorting the Ghost:

If thou hast any sound or use of voice,
Speak to me.

Speak to me. Use words. Construct a language so that I can know what I do not know and what I desperately desire to know. Even before Hamlet appears on the stage, before there can be any reference to the play's many themes and structural patterns (the revenge theme, madness, spying, the lost father, the mother's guilt, the diseased state, the Oedipus Complex, etc.), before we see any of the principal personages of the play, the sentinel Francisco who appears for no more than some three minutes and speaks only fifty-four words has established the theme of language and meaning. *Nay, answer me.* All the major characters will echo that phrase. Francisco also declares, almost casually, 'And I am sick at heart.' He does not tell us why, and we scarcely pay the phrase any attention, for there is no reason for so unimportant a character to be making so portentous a statement; but it is, we soon realise, also Hamlet's condition. *Stand and unfold yourself.* Hamlet could be asking that of language; or of life. From the very beginning of the play, ignorance is a torment. Who can say what is going on?

That can I. The scholar's glib assertion; the easy pretension that learning can be applied to experience and all things satisfactorily explained. Horatio's answer to Marcellus is in a language which nearly parodies the inflated jargon of a young lawyer eager to appear knowledgeable:

> ... this Fortinbras, who, by a sealed compact
> Well ratified by law and heraldry,
> Did forfeit, with his life, all those his lands
> Which he stood seized of, to the conqueror;
> Against the which a moiety competent
> Was gagèd by our King, which had returned
> To the inheritance of Fortinbras,
> Had he been vanquisher, as, by the same comart
> And carriage of the article designed,
> His fell to Hamlet.

Nearly thirty lines of this; at the start of a play, it is hardly
a language calculated to put the audience into the picture.
And what's more, Horatio has just seen a ghost! Not
something that happens every day that one, seeing an
apparition, can coolly resume historical explanation in a
language studded with legal jargon. It is a precise explanation, of course, but poor Marcellus, who had only
asked *tell me he that knows*, must surely find it obscure or
at least long-winded. But Horatio is not finished with
explanation yet, for, a scholar showing off his knowledge,
he embarks upon a parallel between Denmark and Rome
and would have had no reason to stop his exhibitionistic
rhetoric ('the moist star, / Upon whose influence Nep-
tune's empire stands') had the Ghost not mercifully re-
entered the stage. Thus, in two speeches, Shakespeare disposes of the scholar's language: it will not do, it is no
answer to those simple but metaphysically profound
words of Marcellus: *tell me he that knows.*

Horatio's self-assurance, his complete command over a
technically complicated language as well as his mastery
of rhetorical devices, all collapse on the reappearance of
the Ghost. Here is a phenomenon he does not know. His
learning has not prepared him to cope with it. He can
only come up with a hopeful formula. '*If* . . . etc.'

> If thou hast any sound or use of voice,
> Speak to me.
> If there be any good thing to be done
> That may to thee do ease and grace to me,
> Speak to me.

A moment later, his voice calls a little more desperately:

> O, speak!

And appealing to the Ghost a fourth time, he cries

> Speak of it. Stay and speak.

It is the desperation of one who believes that all mysteries
can be solved by rational explanation. Speak and you will
be able to say who you are. Speak and I shall know. It is
a scholar's illusion, of course; or a philosopher's; or a
poet's: that language will reveal.

We have reached line 139 of the play and the second
line, *Nay, answer me. Stand and unfold yourself*, is still
echoing on the stage. As it will continue to echo throughout the play, and the word *speak* will be used again and
again, right to the very last minute of the play when Fortinbras, calling for military honours for Hamlet's dead
body, will ask for 'The soldiers' music and the rite of war'
to

> Speak loudly for him.

The Ghost says nothing. And Horatio, frustrated seeker
after truth who has given the impression of believing that
speech equals explanation, says:

> ... and by my advice
> Let us impart what we have seen tonight
> Unto young Hamlet, for upon my life
> This spirit, dumb to us, will speak to him.

Horatio does not say that the Ghost will speak to Hamlet
because it looks like his late father. Marcellus had said
when the Ghost first appeared.

> Thou art a scholar; speak to it, Horatio.

And Horatio, having failed to receive an answer, now thinks that Hamlet, presumably a greater scholar than himself, will be able to succeed. Hamlet might know how to probe this mystery which his, Horatio's, rhetorical outburst has failed to do: Hamlet might have a better linguistic formula than the nervous cry *Speak to me*.

One learns few facts from the first scene. If there is any foreshadowing of action, it is only to do with young Fortinbras. Otherwise, we see the Ghost of the late king and hear some fancy talk from Horatio. There is little in the substance of the scene which ties up with the many interpretations which have been given the play.

But there is that word *speak* which appears again and again. Before any of the other themes are established, the scene clearly marks out the frontiers of that abstraction which is the ultimate business of literature: to test relationships between language and reality. If we could only hear or speak or arrive at the words which explained, we would *know*; and having the illusion that there is a necessary correspondence between language and reality, we are driven to despair when our words seem to reveal nothing. We are made mad by not knowing. We are left in the end with silence. As is Hamlet whose last word in the play is *silence*.

Hamlet, a play in two words:

Speak.
Silence.

An anguished cry for an answer. There is no answer.

Compare *Breath* by Beckett, a play which takes thirty-five seconds to perform and in which there is the sound of human breath and a human cry and silence. Again, the formula is: *speak*; *silence*.

And Prufrock, who hears too many words within himself:

> Oh, do not ask, 'What is it?'

And John Ashbery in the opening passage of his long prose-poem, *The New Spirit*:

> I thought that if I could put it all down, that would be one way. And next the thought came to me that to leave all out would be another, and truer, way.

Speak; silence.

And Wittgenstein in the last line of his *Tractatus Logico-Philosophicus*:

> Whereof one cannot speak, thereof one must be silent.

Claudius, King of Denmark, complete master of the rhetoric of persuasion, certain of the effect his speech has on his court, speaking in a confident tone which asserts his authority and yet conveys his solicitous concern for the welfare of the state, disposes of his brother's death in $15\frac{1}{2}$ lines of an outrageous playing with shallow phrases which sound impressive to his sycophantic audience—

Have we, as 'twere, with a defeated joy,
With an auspicious and a dropping eye,
With mirth in funeral, and with dirge in marriage, . . .

—and then has the audacity to add, probably in a lowered voice affecting a tragic tone (which at the same time has a dismissive gesture to it, as if to indicate that life, after all, must go on), the hypocritical words: 'For all, our thanks.' It is the consummate performance of a brilliant politician who must use words to maintain and strengthen his power; it is a most *calculated*, cunning use of language, it is pretending to a truth when the substance behind it is a lie. For Claudius, language is only a tool to be used skilfully and not a structure which imposes its subtle forms upon perceptions and renders reality a puzzle, which sometimes creates the illusion of knowledge and sometimes

masquerades as knowledge itself. Claudius has no interest
in conveying a meaning unless it serves his own ends, and
he certainly has no interest in the idea of meaning itself;
as a man of affairs, devoted to worldly ambitions, he can
have no patience with epistemological enquiry. His first
speech is a demonstration to his court that he is an effective
ruler, the state's business is in efficient hands and he is to
be trusted. A progressive new era is about to commence.
To emphasise his understanding of events and his firm
grasp of political reality, he disposes of Fortinbras in nine
lines in which a reference to 'our most valiant brother' is a
nicely calculated phrase which implies a protestation of
innocence, and in which the earlier audacity of 'For all,
our thanks' is matched by the superior attitude implied by
'So much for him.' And like a good, efficient ruler, he sends
off his ambassadors to settle the matter with 'old Norway'.
Everything he says is out to prove that he is very much in
command: he is a man of his word and his word is to be
translated immediately into action. And then, turning
charmingly to Laertes:

> You cannot speak of reason to the Dane
> And lose your voice.

Claudius can listen to practical proposals: speak to him
of the affairs of the world and he will respond with complete understanding: the word *speak* has no menace for
him. Laertes, of course, is a political animal himself, a man
of the same mould as Claudius (just as Horatio is of
Hamlet's): Laertes had come to Denmark, he says, openly
hypocritical, for the coronation (Horatio declares a little
later that he came for the funeral).

Both Laertes and Claudius use language to advance
themselves in the practical realm: meaning is important

only in so far as it creates the right impression. In contrast to them, Hamlet's first line, 'A little more than kin, and less than kind!', spoken as an aside (and therefore not intended to communicate an idea to anyone), is a play on words, an intellectual use of language intended more to gratify himself than to make an impression on his listeners; his last words in the play, 'the rest is silence', are an abandonment of language which has not helped him. But here, in the first scene in which we see him, his concern seems more with appearance and reality and with the meaning and implications of a single word than it is with his father.

> Seems, madam? Nay, it is. I know not 'seems'.

He cannot talk without becoming involved in definitions, in the fine meanings of language. The Queen refers to 'thy noble father' and Claudius talks of 'these mourning duties to your father', but Hamlet himself makes no reference to his father: his language is generalised:

> Seems, madam? Nay, it is. I know not 'seems'.
> 'Tis not alone my inky cloak, good mother,
> Nor customary suits of solemn black,
> Nor windy suspiration of forced breath,
> No, nor the fruitful river in the eye,
> Nor the dejected haviour of the visage,
> Together with all forms, moods, shapes of grief,
> That can denote me truly. These indeed seem,
> For they are actions that a man might play,
> But I have that within which passes show;
> These but the trappings and the suits of woe.

It is a pretentious little speech. Asked a simple question, he answers in the language of metaphysics, using such jargon words as 'forms' and 'denote', and indicates that the inner reality is something other than the outward appearance: it is not a statement which necessarily refers to his immediate situation. It is too abstract for Claudius, who launches upon a long speech of sweet reason, seizing the opportunity to demonstrate to the court a professedly genuine desire to be a loving step-father, and throwing in a couple of lines for the brooding philosopher:

> For what we know must be and is as common
> As any the most vulgar thing to sense,

but Hamlet does not even respond. Truth for him is not so easily reducible to an object of common sense in a language of such simplicity. No wonder his step-father and mother do not want him to return to Wittenburg: Hamlet is too much of a scholar already, what good will his obsession with precise speech, his compulsion to go beyond the mere illusion of meaning suggested by words and to comprehend reality itself, be if he is ever to play a role in the affairs of Denmark?

*　　*　　*

Left alone with his thoughts, Hamlet turns to the thought that torments him: there is no meaning to existence, better to become a drop of dew than carry the burden of sullied flesh.

> How weary, stale, flat, and unprofitable
> Seem to me all the uses of this world!

The *uses*: the practical events, the schemes by which one exists, the ordinary daily responsibilities. It's all worthless. Not because his father is dead and his mother has rushed into marrying the uncle; these are matters concerning ordinary reality which one must somehow endure: they touch one's feelings profoundly and open a wound in the very heart of one's vanity, but they are not *problems* concerning existence; they engender emotional pains but if they touch the intellect at all it is to make it more resolute in determining that the knowledge it possesses can be held to be irrefutably certain. There is no relation between Hamlet's thought and the mundane events in which his body is obliged to dwell. The opening lines of the first soliloquy comprise an abstract statement:

> O that this too too sullied flesh would melt,
> Thaw, and resolve itself into a dew,

and there is no connection between this abstraction and the action which has just taken place. The world which is 'an unweeded garden / That grows to seed' is within Hamlet's mind, and his mind will continue to dwell on that metaphor until he arrives in the graveyard, the one scene in the play where (before the funeral party enters the scene) he is most at peace with himself, where his language is without that turbulence of expression which marks his speeches in so many earlier scenes, and where he can be said to be at home, having found the physical realisation of the symbol which so obsesses his mind.

He turns, in the first soliloquy, to his mother's behaviour as an afterthought. Life intrudes into his world of pure ideas and obliges him to concern himself with the events around him. Existence is meaningless but the petty business of carrying on living has unfortunately to be attended to. The philosopher does philosophy in the seclusion of his study but he's also got to carry the trash-can out for the garbage collectors who come on Monday morning.

Why did Eliot not see that here, in the very first expression of Hamlet's thought, was a formulation of the play's objective correlative? Eliot, one suspects, was looking at the play from a nineteenth-century perspective (for it is still hard to put *character* and psychological *motivation* out of one's mind) and attempting an interpretation by pondering the language which the play did *not* contain. The benefit to mankind has been that in the process of looking for what was missing in *Hamlet*, Eliot hit upon his theory of the 'objective correlative' but, ironically, saw no application of the principle he had discovered to the very thing, looking at which, gave him that principle; it is as if Newton, seeing an apple fall and arriving at the theory of gravity, were then to write an essay describing the remarkable phenomenon of falling apples possessing no gravity. Hamlet simply does not have the sort of emotion that an Othello is given to; his outbursts against Ophelia and his mother are not necessarily emotional, they could be, as we shall see, an expression of a *hatred of life*. The objective formula need not be a correlative of emotions only; it can be a correlative of pure ideas. In Act IV, scene iv, Hamlet is on his way to England and on 'a plain in Denmark' he encounters the Captain to whom Fortinbras has just given some instructions. Hamlet questions the Captain, asking if Fortinbras's army is going to invade the main part of Poland, and the Captain answers

> Truly to speak, and with no addition,
> We go to gain a little patch of ground
> That hath in it no profit but the name.

It is the first time we see Hamlet outside the Castle, and the first thing he runs into is an image of his own unweeded garden! Reality confirms the conclusions of abstract

thought. The next time we see Hamlet it is in the graveyard. There is no getting away from the *little patch of
ground* which is the perfect object which represents the
idea in his mind.

*   *   *

'And what make you from Wittenburg, Horatio?', Hamlet
asks Horatio *twice*: as if astonished that anyone could
want to leave a life devoted to thought and prefer to live
in a royal court.

On hearing Horatio's account of the Ghost, and receiv-
ing to his own anxious question 'Did you not speak to it?'
Horatio's answer that the Ghost had made a 'motion like
as it would speak', Hamlet resolves to 'watch tonight' and
if the Ghost appears again, *he* will 'speak to it . . .'

It is his chance to discover the meaning of life as much
as to find out if there has not been some foul play. There
is the expectation that words will, finally, reveal. Let me
not *burst* in ignorance, he will cry to the Ghost, give me
knowledge, tell me . . . O speak!

This body, that world; and *this dust of words*. And here and there, now and again, a flock of parrots swooping against the sunset on the edge of a rain-forest in the Yucatan, or the ocean bejewelled with islands, each with its halo of white sand, as you fly over the Caribbean, the glimpses of paradise. Perception explodes in instants of inexplicable beauty and desire itself dissolves when it is most unbearable: what is purchased immediately becomes inaccessible:

> In all the argosy of your bright hair I dreamed
> Nothing so flagless as this piracy.
>
> HART CRANE: *Voyages*

The intensity of a vision is measured by the failure of rational language to record it and we are overtaken by conceptions of such subtle deliquescence that we are left contemplating nothing. And the words which we had hoped to pluck from the air to capture the correspondence itself between ideas and reality, between the thought of a vision and vision itself, between propositions and knowledge, the words give nothing but their own sounds, cynically filling the air with reverberations and if we believe we have grasped meaning, it soon sounds hollow.

One lives in a torment of words, trapped by the high hedges of grammar in the labyrinth of language with its million dead-ends but always the promise of a way out:

> . . . it's I am talking, thirsting, starving, let it stand, in the ice and in the furnace, you feel nothing, strange, you don't feel a mouth on you, you don't feel your mouth any more, no need of a mouth, the words are everywhere, inside me, outside me, well well, a minute ago I had no thickness, I hear them, no need to hear them, no need of a head, impossible to stop them, impossible to stop, I'm in words, made of words, others' words, what others, the place too, the air, the walls, the floor, the ceiling, all words, the whole world is here with me, I'm the air, the walls, the walled-in one, everything yields, opens, ebbs, flows, like flakes, I'm all these flakes, meeting, mingling, falling asunder, wherever I go I find me, leave me, go towards me, come from me, nothing ever but me, a particle of me, retrieved, lost, gone astray, I'm all these words, all these strangers, this dust of words, . . .
>
> BECKETT: *The Unnamable*

A father's death, a mother's hasty remarriage are nothing compared to the agony of Nothing.

> Except that the silence continues to focus on you. Who am I after all, you say despairingly once again, to have merited so much attention on the part of the universe; what does it think to get from me that it doesn't have already? I know too that my solipsistic approach is totally wrong-headed and foolish, that the universe isn't listening to me any more than the sea can be heard inside conch shells.
>
> JOHN ASHBERY: The System

And Wallace Stevens in *The Idea of Order at Key West*:

> Oh! Blessed rage for order, pale Ramon,
> The maker's rage to order words of the sea,
> Words of the fragrant portals, dimly-starred,
> And of ourselves and of our origins,
> In ghostlier demarcations, keener sounds.

So much of twentieth-century literature seems to be an attempt to write new soliloquies for Hamlet.

LAERTES: Farewell, Ophelia, and remember well
What I have said to you.
OPHELIA: 'Tis in my memory locked,
And you yourself shall keep the key of it.
LAERTES: Farewell. (*Exit* LAERTES)

And in the very next moment when Polonius asks, 'What is't, Ophelia, he hath said to you?', she blurts it all out. For one who has *locked* a secret and given away the key to the now-departed brother, she does not hesitate for a second: thus, the very first thing we see about Ophelia is the way in which she contradicts her own words.

She uses language absent-mindedly, speaking phrases which are neat, sometimes poetically elegant structures, but there is not always a true understanding within her of what she has said. She merely goes through the motions of rationality. When she immediately gives away her secret, she does so not simply because she is an obedient daughter and Polonius an authoritarian father, for she could easily have lied – sisters do share secrets with their brothers about which they lie to their parents. No, Ophelia simply does not understand the words she uses, and if it can be said that our knowledge of the world is a measure of the language we understand, then she has no grasp over reality; which is why it is logical that she should lose all hold over reality and go mad. (And in her madness sing: pure lyrics, those stunning combinations of words which reveal truth that is beyond apparent reality: for it is in her madness that she says, 'Pray let's have no words of this, but when they ask you what it means, say you this' – and then bursts into song. And Hamlet, following his feigned madness, will write a few lines to interpolate into the play within the play to see if the language of fiction, which is as much a lie as the language of madness as far as the so-called 'real' world is concerned, will not reveal a truth). So, beginning with the opening lines of the first scene in which she appears, Ophelia's language is seen to be irresponsible; she speaks words without knowing what she is saying; and the vagueness of her speech is indicative of the vagueness of her perception. Polonius is being literally precise when he admonishes her with, 'You do not understand yourself so clearly', and little does she herself realise the subtly self-reflexive irony of 'I do not know, my lord, what I should think.'

Polonius, offering to teach her, plays upon the word 'tenders' and is compelled to add parenthetically, '(not to crack the wind of the poor phrase' – the compulsive aside of one obsessed by linguistic niceties; he is closest to Hamlet in his use of language, going so far as to comment upon the precise use of words ('That's good, "Mobled queen" is good.'), for he too wants to get to the bottom of things. But unlike Hamlet, his interest in language, while it has its academic and abstract moments, is utilitarian; for him, language is an instrument of discoveries to do with human behaviour. When Ophelia tells him of Hamlet's declarations of love, Polonius dismisses them, suggesting that Hamlet's 'holy vows' are only words, they represent

no meaning – and he knows the corruption that comes
from the use of empty words.

> Do not believe his vows, for they are brokers,
> Not of that dye which their investments show,
> But mere implorators of unholy suits,
> Breathing like sanctified and pious bawds,
> The better to beguile. This is for all:
> I would not, in plain terms, from this time forth
> Have you so slander any moment leisure
> As to give words or talk with the Lord Hamlet.

– forbidding her to *speak* and thereby reveal knowledge
about herself. Having expressed the idea, he needs to repeat
it *in plain terms* to make sure Ophelia understands. And
in forbidding Ophelia 'to give words or talk with the Lord
Hamlet', Polonius perhaps fears that Hamlet with his
superior mastery of language would not only ensnare
Ophelia (for his holy vows are but 'springes to catch wood-
cocks') but also, and this would surely be worse, Hamlet
might perceive Ophelia's essential stupidity and should
the prince indeed be in love with her, possibly change his
mind when he observes her dull mind. The protection of
Ophelia's chastity is a good excuse to keep her away from
the man who would be wonderful to have as her husband
but who, given any sort of prolonged premarital intimacy,
even an innocuous one, is bound to see the vapidity of her
brain. 'I shall obey, my lord' is the dutiful answer; and the
answer also of one who can respond only in trite phrases.
The situations in which Ophelia appears before she goes
mad are too complex for her understanding; and the language she hears from her father and from Hamlet is invariably beyond her and each is obliged to say something
simple in order to get a response from her. In her meek

conformity, she lives in a meaningless world until her madness relieves her of the responsibility to language and she can ignore the speech of everyone else and herself speak what gibberish comes to her mind: and in that total collapse of the relationship between language and reality, see visions.

Enter the Ghost again, and Hamlet cries out, 'Thou com'st in such a questionable shape / That I will speak to thee.' And then desperately,

> . . . O, answer me!
> Let me not burst in ignorance . . .

The violence inherent in 'burst' tells us something of his mental anguish. 'What may this mean?', he pleads; has the Ghost come 'With thoughts beyond the reaches of our souls'? All the pain of not knowing that has been growing within him bursts as he shouts:

> Say, why is this? Wherefore? What should we do?

And when Hamlet decides to follow the Ghost, his first reason is not that the Ghost beckons him, but that it is silent:

> It will not speak. Then I will follow it.

The positioning of 'Then' is determined by more than the necessities of metre; and more than the sound of the line depends on where that 'Then' is positioned. It takes one right back to the opening of the play: *Nay, answer me. Stand and unfold yourself.*

GHOST: Pity me not, but lend thy serious hearing
              To what I shall unfold.
HAMLET: Speak. I am bound to hear.

But what the Ghost unfolds is not knowledge; he tells Hamlet nothing of the 'thoughts beyond the reaches of our souls'; but gives only an account of how he, as Hamlet's father, had been killed by Claudius. The Ghost, who might have revealed the answers to all of Hamlet's metaphysical questions and made language redundant by providing the son with a vision into ultimate truth, can only talk at the petty level of his own former miserable vanity. (And incidentally, we have only the Ghost's word, and Hamlet's biased judgement, for the former King's merits. The Ghost says:

> O Hamlet, what a falling-off was there,
> From me, whose love was of that dignity
> That it went hand in hand even with the vow
> I made to her in marriage, and to decline
> Upon a wretch whose natural gifts were poor
> To those of mine.

It sounds very much like the resentment of an elder brother at the younger brother being cleverer, for we have no evidence that the former King was in fact superior to Claudius. Certainly, after Claudius's performance in Act I, scene ii, it is difficult to imagine a shrewder head of state; whereas Hamlet's father seems to have been given over to luxury and indolence. And all he wants now, as a Ghost, is vengeance, i.e. a placating of his own vanity.)

The Ghost has only an earthly story to tell, melo-dramatic and self-pitying at that, and anticipates Hamlet's metaphysical curiosity by saying, 'But that I am forbid / To tell the secrets of my prison house . . .', so that Hamlet has no choice but to listen to words pertaining only to mundane events.

Horatio and Marcellus come in search of Hamlet after his encounter with the Ghost and when they ask him for an explanation, he can only give them what Horatio bitterly calls 'wild and whirling words'. Poor Horatio: the Ghost, in the first scene, had not answered his *Speak to me* and now Hamlet, from whom he can reasonably expect an answer, will not speak either though his question is still, desperately, the same.

It is Hamlet's 'cursèd spite' to revenge his father's death. He would rather not be in this world which demands action, and it would have been easier for him if the Ghost had only given an intellectually interesting account of life after death. Instead, the Ghost has said nothing about death, and therefore revealed nothing about life, but merely talked about his own dying. In his emotional outburst at hearing the Ghost's story, Hamlet makes a solemn resolution:

> Yea, from the table of my memory
> I'll wipe away all trivial fond records,
> All saws of books, all forms, all pressures past
> That youth and observation copied there,
> And thy commandment all alone shall live
> Within the book and volume of my brain,
> Unmixed with baser matter. Yes, by heaven!

It is only the heat of the moment, however, for the next time we see Hamlet, in Act II, scene ii, he enters the stage, the stage-direction informs us, *reading on a book*.

Speak. Tell. Answer me. Consider the opening lines of the
twenty scenes of *Hamlet.*

BERNARDO: Who's there?
FRANCISCO: Nay, *answer me.* Stand and *unfold your-
            self.*   Act I, scene i

                    *   *   *

CLAUDIUS: Though yet of Hamlet our dear brother's
            death . . .
                                            Act I, scene ii
                    *   *   *

LAERTES: My necessaries are embarked. Farewell.
            And, sister, as the winds give benefit
            And convoy is assistant, do not sleep,
            But *let me hear* from you.
                                            Act I, scene iii
                    *   *   *

HAMLET: The air bites shrewdly; it is very cold.
HORATIO: It is a nipping and an eager air.
HAMLET: What hour now?

HORATIO:　　　　　　　　　I think it lacks of twelve.

MARCELLUS:　No, it is struck.

HORATIO:　Indeed? I heard it not. It then draws near the season

Wherein the spirit held his wont to walk.

(*A flourish of trumpets, and two pieces go off.*)
What does this mean, my lord?

Act I, scene iv

*　　*　　*

HAMLET:　Whither wilt thou lead me? *Speak*; I'll go no further.

Act I, scene v

*　　*　　*

POLONIUS:　Give him this money and these notes, Reynaldo.

REYNALDO:　I will, my lord.

POLONIUS:　You shall do marvell's wisely, good Reynaldo,

Before you visit him, to make *inquire*
Of his behaviour.

Act II, scene i

*　　*　　*

KING:　Welcome, dear Rosencrantz and Guildenstern.

Act II, scene ii

*　　*　　*

KING:　And can you *by no drift of conference Get* from him why he puts on this confusion ...

Act III, scene i

*　　*　　*

HAMLET: *Speak* the speech, I pray you . . .
                              Act III, scene ii

          *   *   *

KING: I like him not, nor stands it safe with
           us . . .
                              Act III, scene iii

          *   *   *

POLONIUS: 'A will come straight. Look you lay home
           to him.
           Tell him his pranks have been too broad
           to bear with . . .
                              Act III, scene iv

          *   *   *

KING: There's matter in these sighs. These pro-
           found heaves
           You must translate; 'tis fit we understand
           them.
                              Act IV, scene i

          *   *   *

HAMLET: Safely stowed.
GENTLEMEN (*within*): Hamlet! Lord Hamlet!
HAMLET: But soft, what noise? Who calls on
           Hamlet?
                              Act IV, scene ii

          *   *   *

KING: I have sent to seek him out and to find the
           body . . .
                              Act IV, scene iii

          *   *   *

FORTINBRAS: Go, Captain from me greet the Danish king.

Tell him that . . .

Act IV, scene iv

* * *

QUEEN: I will not *speak* with her.

Act IV, scene v

* * *

HORATIO: What are they that would *speak* with me?

Act IV, scene vi

* * *

KING: Now must your conscience my acquittance seal,

And you must put me in your heart for friend,

Sith you have *heard*, and with a knowing ear . . .

Act IV, scene vii

* * *

CLOWN: Is she to be buried in Christian burial when she wilfully seeks her own salvaation?

OTHER: I *tell* thee she is.

Act V, scene i

* * *

HAMLET: So much for this, sir, now shall you *see* the other.

Act V, scene ii

* * *

In these opening lines of the twenty scenes, again and again there is some statement to do with a desire to know, to impart information or to discover some fact. Only four of the scenes (I, ii; II, ii; III, iii; and IV, iii) do not express someone's anxiety to speak or to hear or to want to know what the words mean.

Polonius's instructions to Reynaldo (Act II, scene i: a scene about which Eliot remarks 'for which there is little excuse') comprise an example of how language can be corrupted so that one can give the impression of telling the truth without actually doing so and, at the same time, without telling a lie. Language, we are to deduce, is not to be trusted; if we can utter propositions which have only the appearance of truth, and yet we ourselves know that they are not necessarily true, and which are not lies either, then what is language if not merely an *idea* in our minds, a structure which we accept or reject depending upon the beliefs we hold? (And Wittgenstein says: 'At the foundation of well-founded belief lies belief that is not founded.' – *On Certainty.*)We cannot depend upon the words we use to contain the truth we like to believe they do because we ourselves can put the same words to corrupt usage: therefore, how can we expect *language* to tell us anything about reality?

Reynaldo is to find 'By this encompassment and drift of question' and not by honest enquiry; he is to be ambiguous, subtle, suggestive; he is to put words into the mouths of the Danes in Paris in order to discover what Laertes is up to: Reynaldo is to carry out an elaborate deception but by using words which have only the semblance of truth. Reynaldo is to 'put on him / What forgeries you please'. Polonius sums it up neatly: 'By indirections find directions out.'

If Laertes is indeed the scoundrel which the 'forgeries' will portray him to be, then they will not be 'forgeries' at all but accurate descriptions which everyone will recognise to be true; and the implication is that should Laertes actually be an upright man and a dutiful son keeping to his father's precepts, then Reynaldo can always say that he was thinking of someone else, it has been a case of mistaken identity: *in either event*, language would appear to have been used to utter truth: and that in itself is the underlying lie behind Polonius's scheme which he spells out to Reynaldo by giving him examples of sentences he should use:

> 'And in part him, but,' you may say, 'not well,
> But if't be he I mean, he's very wild,
> Addicted so and so.' And there put on him
> What forgeries you please; . . .

Polonius is both a statesman and a scholar. He is sharper than Claudius in his understanding of language as a tool to serve a political end; he also understands language as a thing in itself, and in this respect he is intellectually superior to Hamlet whose word-games are almost a mockery of himself and who, like a writer, like Beckett, say, is trapped by language, finding an endless necessity to use words and never being able to know the world behind those words, being obliged merely to carry on experiments in grammar, while for Polonius language is never without a practical use. If the two men had literary careers, Hamlet would be a poet, Polonius a critic.

Eliot did not see the relevance of the Reynaldo scene

because he was looking at the play's action and the psychological motivation of its characters and, surprisingly for so great a poet, not looking at the language. In his essay, Eliot is dismissive of Horatio's famous

> But look, the morn in russet mantle clad
> Walks o'er the dew of yon high eastern hill,

because it reminds him of the relatively immature Shakespeare of *Romeo and Juliet* but, as noted before, Horatio in the same scene (I, i.) also uses the language of a keen young lawyer, and if we observe that one of the central preoccupations of the play is to use examples of speech to indicate the quality of the speaker's mind and his understanding of reality, then surely Horatio's 'russet mantle clad' is perfectly acceptable as showing that Horatio, a scholar, is over-impressed by certain types of expression and loses no opportunity to use them, especially among people who are intellectually his inferiors. It is an affectation common to young people who have recently come down from a university. We are the victims of the language we have learned, especially when we believe that that language has liberated our minds and given us the freedom to observe the world as it really is, which, of course, is a nice illusion since we do not observe that the language of our emancipation itself consists of chains of words with the only difference that they are of another complexity than we had comprehended before. Far from being a scene for which there is little excuse, the Polonius-Reynaldo scene is a neatly objectified dramatisation which correlates very precisely with the play's larger theme of language. As do the speeches concerning the Players and Hamlet's instructions on how to speak a speech.

*   *   *

In the same scene is Ophelia's description of Hamlet coming to her in an incredibly distracted manner. She says to her father:

> My lord, as I was sewing in my closet,
> Lord Hamlet, with his doublet all unbraced,
> No hat upon his head, his stockings fouled,
> Ungartered, and down-gyvèd to his ankle,
> Pale as his shirt, his knees knocking each other,
> And with a look so piteous in purport,
> As if he had been loosèd out of hell
> To speak of horrors – he comes before me.

It is bizarre behaviour, to say the least, and it could be that this has been one of Hamlet's first attempts to show himself as being mad, but I doubt it. In fact, I doubt Ophelia's words. The image of Hamlet, 'his knees knocking each other' and the rest of Ophelia's description, is too fanciful to be believed, for there is nothing else in the play to suggest that Hamlet attempts to advertise his madness in any other way than through a manipulation of language. If he seriously loves Ophelia (as he later declares in the graveyard scene that he did), he is not going to appear to her in the guise of a demented fool; and if his interest is only to seduce her, then his technique is going to be subtler than simply dropping his stockings to his ankles. No. Instead of an image of Hamlet's feigned madness, what we have here is a foreshadowing of Ophelia's own madness. Her mind is inventing an unreality, and she is scared: she does preface her description by saying to her father:

> O my lord, my lord, I have been so affrighted!

The irony is that Polonius does not see the symptoms of madness in his daughter but instead, translating her words according to his own beliefs, immediately concludes that Hamlet has been driven to distraction by love for his daughter. It is a perfect example of how when someone does *speak* to us, we hear something else. We are interpreters and translators of what we hear and understand only that which accords with our beliefs. There is no reason to doubt anyone whose speech does not violate the rules of grammar.

'More matter, with less art', implores the Queen: to which Polonius answers

> Madam, I swear I use no art at all.
> That he is mad, 'tis true: 'tis true 'tis pity,
> And pity 'tis 'tis true – a foolish figure.
> But farewell it, for I will use no art.

Speak clearly, tell us what you really mean: that is the simple-minded person's cry while the scholarly mind, trying hard to say precisely what it means, becomes involved in labyrinthine phrases and protests that it is only saying what in fact is the case; and such a mind is also so obsessive an analyst of the structure of its own language that it often compulsively comments (in an aside) upon the form of words it is in the process of uttering.

Polonius is not so much a long-winded fool, which he is sometimes represented to be, as a mind which is torn between wanting to use a complex language in order to communicate precisely the complexity of ideas while being aware, at the same time, that to most other minds such seemingly convoluted formulae seem bizarre, and so will have a self-critical aside ('a foolish figure') or add a re-assuring phrase at the end of a complicated sentence ('I will be brief.'). He comments compulsively not only upon his own but also upon others' language, as has been observed with his remark upon the 'mobled' queen, and when he reads Hamlet's letter to Ophelia he cannot resist remarking on one of Hamlet's phrases: 'That's an ill phrase, a vile phrase; "beautified" is a vile phrase.'

Who cares? Certainly not Claudius and the Queen, who are only interested in the *matter* of Hamlet's letter and not in its *art*. It is this sort of aside which has made many actors interpret Polonius as a lovable old imbecile, provoking an easy mirth among audiences, thereby missing the point that what Shakespeare is doing is to focus attention upon the way in which language is used. There is nothing of the old fool in Polonius when he says

> If circumstances lead me, I will find
> Where truth is hid, though it were hid indeed
> Within the centre.

Unlike Hamlet, however, his interest in language is not allied to a quest for knowledge, for Polonius seems to have concluded already that we can know nothing:

> My liege and madam, to expostulate
> What majesty should be, what duty is,
> Why day is day, night night, and time is time,
> Were nothing but to waste night, day, and time.

It is futile to speculate about things and abstractions. But yet language offers a scope for speculation, and Polonius turns that upon language itself, deriving pleasure from a fine phrase.

*   *   *

And now: '*Enter* HAMLET *reading on a book.*'

QUEEN: But look where sadly the poor wretch comes reading.

The poor wretch has gone mad, apparently, but the audience knows it is only a feigned madness. It is difficult for the modern audience not to be aware of some three hundred-odd years of criticism which has tried to account for this madness. Even Eliot talks about it: 'For Shakespeare it is less than madness and more than feigned. The levity of Hamlet, his repetition of phrase, his puns, are not part of a deliberate plan of dissimulation, but a form of emotional relief.' Eliot is again looking at psychology and not at language (and, incidentally, Eliot's own language sounds more impressive than the meaning it conveys: that first sentence seems to have been prompted by a desire to utter paradox. Sometimes, a neatness of phraseology convinces us that we have said something remarkable.)

But we do have a mad person in the play, Ophelia, and her madness is represented as a failure of language to be rational: words used with no seeming logic. Of course, at the literal level of the play's action, whether we see it as merely a revenge tragedy or as containing one or more of the many other themes, such as spying, the reasons for Hamlet's feigned madness are obvious enough: he does not want to seem to appear responsible, he wants the freedom to observe for as a madman he can be in places where his presence would otherwise be suspicious to the King, etc. But if we pursue the theme of language, then the feigned madness is explicable in an entirely different way.

One thing which distinguishes mad people from the sane is that they have no hold over language. Rational speech is an attempt to communicate and to understand meaning and there is a tacit assumption between the sender and the receiver of a message that they both speak 'the same language'. Words tell us not only what a thing is but also what is behind it, how it is to be interpreted. Also, language is our tool of epistemological enquiry, we attempt to comprehend the objects of experience through words. But no philosopher has ever been able to come up with a final theory of knowledge because each has ended by constructing only a new combination of words. In the end, there are only words; and a grammar to govern the usage of those words, a grammar which human beings themselves have invented in the first place. We live in a chaos of sentences, kept sane by grammar's illusion of order.

Compare Wittgenstein:

> 'I can't be making a mistake' is an ordinary sentence, which serves to give the certainty-value of a statement. And only in its everyday use is it justified.
>
> But what the devil use is it if – as everyone admits – I may be wrong about it, and therefore about the proposition it was supposed to support too?
>
> Or shall I say: the sentence excludes a certain *kind* of failure?
>
> *On Certainty*

Like Beckett's characters, we are finally condemned to muttering endless sequences of words with no hope of arriving at a meaning that penetrates the barrier of language. Our excursions into the sciences show us other barriers rather than reveal knowledge. Beckett in *Molloy*:

> Yes, I once took an interest in astronomy, I don't deny it. Then it was geology that killed a few years for me. The next pain in the balls was anthropology and the other disciplines, such as psychiatry, that are connected with it, disconnected, then connected again, according

to the latest discoveries. What I liked in anthropology was its inexhaustible faculty of negation, its relentless definition of man, as though he were no better than God, in terms of what he is not. But my ideas on this subject were always horribly confused, for my knowledge of men was scant and the meaning of being beyond me. Oh I've tried everything.

We are left muttering to ourselves. *Stultior stultissimo –* Beckett's memorable phrase.

Once the realisation strikes one's mind that no language-proposition is ever going to represent a true perception of reality, then one is confronted by the ultimate failure of the human intellect. What can one do? Let us experiment, let us reverse our normal procedure. Instead of expecting words to be rational, neatly continuing the attractive formula of cause and effect, let us see what happens when the words are exaggeratedly irrational and blatantly nonsensical. As in the drama of Jarry and Ionesco. Sanity has not given us the truth we seek, let us attempt insanity. Rational language has not helped us, it stubbornly refuses to tell us anything about life and even the dead father, returning as a ghost, cannot enlighten the son who is obliged to resume reading his books. So, let us, as scientists do, submit our propositions to a deliberate contradiction, apply the test of the negative, examine anti-meaning (just as some modern poets have written anti-poems in order to write meaningful poems which they have believed no longer possible by using the linguistic procedures of tra-ditional forms) and see if a deliberate confusion will not create a new order in one's mind.

Speak and *silence*. And in between a feigned madness, an experiment in speech calculated to do the opposite of *unfolding* oneself to see if anti-language will not do what language consistently fails to do. Listen again to Lucky's speech in *Waiting for Godot*, that violently rapid and maddened flow of words at the heart of the play, to see how the writer needs to tear at language in the desperate rage for meaning. Or observe how the language of *Waiting for Godot*, an early play, becomes a silence in *Breath*, a late play, or how the compulsive rationality in *Murphy* and *Watt*, the first two novels, gives way in *Lessness*, a late fiction, to an attempt to deny grammar its traditional role. The collected works of Samuel Beckett can be said to take place within the mind of Hamlet, Prince of Denmark; and the seemingly irrational language of the later works, such as *How It Is* and *Lessness*, is a sort of feigned madness which, when one begins to make connections, seem truer in their comprehension of reality than the earlier, seemingly rational works. Beckett is not the only writer to have applied the technique of apparent logical irresponsibility. T. S. Eliot did so. Indeed, apparent literal incoherence has been so common in twentieth-century literature that we accept it as a valid technique and are more inclined to raise our eyebrows at simple, direct expression. Hamlet's madness, projected primarily through language, while it serves the action at a literal level, is also an experiment in language. And the play *Hamlet*, it seems to me, is the objective correlative of literature.

*   *   *

The Waste Land is, at one level, a quest for meaning in which the poet founders among languages and literatures and even when he arrives at the end to the illusion of understanding and resolution provided by the hypnotic Sanskrit formula, he has scarcely emerged from the deliberate violence to rationality suggested by 'Why then Ile fit you. Hieronymo's mad againe.' In this quest, the poet's language suffers repeated breakdowns and adumbrates a methodical madness to see if a juxtaposition of fragments, each with its visionary gleam, will not come together as a finally revealing brightness. And

> Here is no water but only rock
> Rock and no water and the sandy road

is Eliot's 'little patch of ground'. There is, in *Hamlet* and in *The Waste Land*, the pursuit of unobtainable vision: the poet is left with only words to mutter and the peace he discovers 'passeth understanding', which is to say, words cannot be used to come to a knowledge of it. There is only silence.

*   *   *

Visions and revisions. Young T. S. Eliot, a scholar engaged in the study of philosophy, fascinated by mystical experience, attending Bergson's lectures during a stay in Paris, his studies ranging from what Harvard had to offer to his purchasing books on Vedanta, wrote 'The Love Song of J. Alfred Prufrock' in 1911 and went on to commence his doctoral thesis, *Experience and the Objects of Knowledge in the Philosophy of F. H. Bradley* in 1913. It is as if in a wilderness of ideas there were suddenly to be a spring of clear water which while being its own self could not help reflecting the world surrounding it. The poet assimilates the ideas of philosophy in his poem in which his own conscious concern might have been entirely unphilosophical and with an astonishing prescience anticipates Bradley's thought. In its quest for the timeless moment, in its passion for unobtainable vision, themes which will not let Eliot alone until he reaches the serenity of 'East Coker', 'Prufrock' begins with a quotation from Dante which has been translated as

> If I thought that my response would be addressed to one who might go back alive, this flame would shake no more; but since no one ever goes back alive out of these deeps (if what I hear is true), without fear of infamy I answer you.

There is to be no Ghost in the poem. We are about to be given an answer from the after-life but the quotation stops there, the Ghost is locked in the epigraph, and Eliot commences his poem:

> Let us go then, you and I,
> When the evening is spread out against the sky
> Like a patient etherised upon a table;

a *modern* image, we applauded when we first saw the poem, approving the poet's twentieth-century awareness, but missed the significance of the *etherised* patient. He is unconscious; which is to say, he has been deprived of the faculty to perceive reality. The poem develops into a counterpointing of the insistence of the objects of knowledge to appear in our consciousness as sensory data and the intellectual despair of being unable to distinguish them from mere appearances.

> Oh, do not ask, 'What is it?'
> Let us go and make our visit.

is the first statement rejecting the compulsion to seek meaning, with the adjuration that one should simply act, or be.

> In the room the women come and go
> Talking of Michelangelo.

There is an assurance in their voice: as if they *know* what they are talking about. Yet 'Michelangelo' exists only as an *idea*; the name does not represent an object of experience, only an object of the human imagination. We can talk of 'Michelangelo' whether or not we know of his life or work, for the habits of language (seeing or hearing a proper name in a grammatically correct sentence) persuade us that we do understand; we can utter sentences about 'Michelangelo' and give the impression of sensible speech even if we are totally ignorant of the reality represented by 'Michelangelo'. Eliot only tells us that the women are 'Talking of Michelangelo'. We are not told what they are saying about him. It would be ridiculous to suggest, though it is not inconceivable, that one of the women might be saying, 'Michelangelo was a Sicilian peasant who emigrated to America in 1892.' For all we know is that the women are making sentences about 'Michelangelo'; the rest is our presumption – though, of course, it would be foolish to believe that the reference is not to the great artist.

But experience insists that it be observed.

> The yellow fog that rubs its back upon the window-
>   panes,
> The yellow smoke that rubs its muzzle on the window-
>   panes,
> Licked its tongue into the corners of the evening,
> Lingered upon the pools that stand in drains,
> Let fall upon its back the soot that falls from chimneys,
> Slipped by the terrace, made a sudden leap,
> And seeing that it was a soft October night,
> Curled once about the house, and fell asleep.

We do not, however, see experience for what it is; even in the act of regarding it, we become engaged in some habit or the other of language and are also distracted by peripheral matter. Here, the object is 'fog' and the words describing the experience of the fog are about a 'cat': what we *see* is a literary use of words, the working out of an extended metaphor, which is pleasing in itself and which conveys the idea of the fog but every time we try to look at the fog we end up by staring at a cat. Metaphor takes us to the heart of the paradox: it creates elaborate, and sometimes intensely beautiful, lies in an attempt to convey truth, but in the end is only itself, a metaphor, a figure of speech. And Language itself is metaphor, a cat that curls about our brains which will not let us know the reality called fog.

There will be time

> . . . for a hundred visions and revisions,
> Before the taking of a toast and tea.

Visions and revisions. The portentous preoccupations of the mind. The taking of a toast and tea. The trivial details which the body has to attend to. (One is reminded of a dominant theme in Chekhov: Life promises the illusion of beautiful existence but living involves us in trivial actions.)

The questions begin. 'Do I dare?' Time and the universe come to Prufrock's mind; and his body of which he notes the outer surfaces:

My morning coat, my collar mounting firmly to the chin,
My necktie rich and modest, but asserted by a simple pin –

not even the outer surfaces, only the clothed generality of man; not he but others will make statements about his thinning hair and thin arms and legs: others will interpret his reality. He himself breaks off from that stream of thought to utter the first of his despairing cries:

For I have known them all already, known them all –
Have known the evenings, mornings, afternoons,
I have measured out my life with coffee spoons;
I know the voices dying with a dying fall
Beneath the music from a farther room.
So how should I presume?

Known is repeated again and again. Prufrock's preoccupation is now entirely epistemological: he has experienced the objects of knowledge, he has been aware of Time and the relative smallness of his own life, he has heard the voices which have indicated a world outside his body, but how should he *presume* to turn all these data into certain knowledge? How should he presume even when he is 'formulated, sprawling on a pin' (like an insect specimen with its label, looking at which and reading the words leads us to conclude that we *know* the insect)? As soon as he makes the assumption that he has known something, 'Arms that are braceleted and white and bare', that knowledge is confounded by a contradictory perception, '(But in the lamplight, downed with light brown hair!)'.

Cf. Bradley: 'The thing, to be at all, must be the same after a change, and the change must, to some extent, be predicated of the thing.'

Cf. also a proposition like Eliot's 'Arms that are . . .' with G. E. Moore's 'Here is one hand . . .'. In his *Proof of an External World*, Moore writes: 'Obviously, then, there are thousands of different things such that, if, at any time, I can prove any one of them, I shall have proved the existence of things outside of us. Cannot I prove any of these things? . . . I can prove now, for instance, that two human hands exist. How? By holding up my two hands, and saying, as I make a certain gesture with the right hand, "Here is one hand", and adding, as I make a certain gesture with the left, "and here is another".'

Cf. also Beckett in *Molloy*: 'And when I see my hands, on the sheet, which they love to floccillate already, they are not mine, less than ever mine, I have no arms . . .' And Prufrock: 'And I have known the arms already, known them all – '.

Shall I say . . . ? Should I make up a sentence (such as 'I have gone at dusk through narrow streets, etc.') and expect the assertion to have meaning? It remains a rhetorical question in Prufrock's mind, for his mind abandons the image to utter a desperate wish:

> I should have been a pair of ragged claws
> Scuttling across the floors of silent seas.

O to be relieved of this desire for knowledge: to be a creature only of instinct in a dark world where there is no perception to torment the mind!

But the world around him continues to present an illusion of its seemingly perfect existence: 'And the afternoon, the evening, sleeps so peacefully!' And while the mind beholds a perspective of contentment, the body is obliged to dwell among trivial things – tea and cakes and ices; the beautiful vision which one is almost about to see vanishes because the ordinary objects of experience distract. It is as if one looked at a blue sky of such a dazzling intensity that it seemed to promise the present appearance of winged horses drawing a golden chariot; instead, a swarm of locusts blots out the blue. Little objects fill one's perception (cf. 'To restore silence is the role of objects.' –

Molloy). Neither the mystic's preparations ('I have wept and fasted, wept and prayed') to make himself receptive to visions nor an identification with a figure of Christian mythology reveals the truth for which Prufrock's mind craves. Instead, *things* come tumbling into his consciousness:

> After the cups, the marmalade, the tea,
> Among the porcelain . . .

bits and pieces are all he can know of the universe and it is futile for him to wish to be like one who has returned from the dead, fully enlightened, 'Come back to tell you all', for most assuredly he has not, being still obliged to be the witness of 'the sunsets and the dooryards and the sprinkled streets', surrounded by novels and teacups and 'the skirts that trail along the floor', and he can only break off the endless list of things in utter exhaustion:

> It is impossible to say just what I mean!

Then follows the reference to Hamlet and it is not certain whether one should take the phrase 'I am not Prince Hamlet' literally or with a measure of irony, but the more one ponders the language of 'Prufrock' and of *Hamlet* the more one observes a striking congruence of thought. In the end of 'Prufrock', the mind, having failed to perceive the vision it has sought, invents one for itself; and to have heard mermaids singing is to have experienced a madness that may or may not have been feigned; the mind, unable to arrive at philosophical truth, turns to the world of pure fiction to see if reality may not be discovered through the formulations of fiction.

As does Hamlet: '*Enter the* PLAYERS.'

Hamlet's encounter with Polonius has been all word-play and one need only quote in passing Polonius's question, 'What do you read, my lord?', and Hamlet's answer, 'Words, words, words', which a twentieth-century philosopher will surely agree is a much more precise answer than if Hamlet had said, 'Beowulf'.

More word-games follow with Rosencrantz and Guildenstern. Indeed, Act II, scene ii, the longest in the play, has examples of the various types of language used in *Hamlet*: from the King's statesmanlike words of dissimulation and the Queen's insipid simple-person's speech to the exchange of wit between Hamlet and Rosencrantz and Guildenstern, including the seeming distortions of language induced by the feigned madness; going on to the language of fiction when Hamlet recalls a speech from a play; and ending with a soliloquy in which Hamlet at last seems to confront his problem but finds a reason to defer its solution a little longer.

Hamlet's excitement at seeing the Players is cerebral; it is not merely a love of the theatre, nor is it due to the realisation that he can use the Players to test the guilt or innocence of the King: his excitement at first is that of one who is fascinated by a stylised literary language. 'I heard thee speak me a speech once, but it was never

acted . . .' How delicious to hear a language which creates
its own indubitable truth which, having been 'never acted,'
has remained locked in itself and which has not suffered
the violence of being subjected to the test of vulgar experience!

There is a genuine spontaneity to Hamlet's excitement:
'You are welcome, masters, welcome, all. I am glad to see
thee well. Welcome, good friends.' And without waiting
for the formality of the Players responding to his greeting,
he says, 'We'll have a speech straight. Come, give us a
taste of your quality. Come, a passionate speech.'

He cannot wait to hear words which create complete
structures of meaning without reference to personal experience. A poem, a sonnet by Shakespeare, say, or a
soliloquy in a play called *Hamlet*, for example, can be
just such a structure constructed on formal principles of
aesthetics or of rhetoric, bounded, that is, by the rules of its
own grammar and yet not confined within any space,
being timeless and immortal unlike the human body and
therefore seeming to possess an access to truth which remains inevitably elusive to common experience. Artistic
formulations have a potential for perfection not available
to ordinary existence\where we must suffer from colds and
constipation; but since in literature the formulations are
made up of words which also belong to ordinary existence,
we are therefore driven to believe that language ought to
allow us visions to do with our own lives which in literature
it does to the abstract concept of Life. And is not the in-
ability to distinguish between these two languages sometimes a source of madness – hallucinations, schizophrenia,
delusions of the self? A mad Ophelia is as much a
visionary as Blake, singing songs the language of which
has transcended common experience.

The speech Hamlet wants to hear is from a play which

too good to be a popular success, it was, he says, 'an excellent play, well digested in the scenes, set down with as much modesty as cunning. I remember one said there were no sallets in the lines to make the matter savoury; nor no matter in the phrase that might indict the author of affectation, but called it an honest method, as whole-some as sweet, and by very much more handsome than fine.'

Here is Hamlet with all manner of private problems, who has recently seen his father's Ghost and who has been pretending to be mad, going on and on about the art of drama. But it is not merely that Shakespeare is giving his contemporaries a lesson in the 'honest method' of his art (and that is not an uncommon practice among writers: see, for example, the novels of Alain Robbe-Grillet, especially *Jealousy*, in which Robbe-Grillet makes two of his characters discuss a novel by contrast with which, it is implied, the novel in Robbe-Grillet's reader's hands is the one with the 'honest method'). And it is not merely that Hamlet's mind has quickly seized the idea that here is a chance to put reality to the test of fiction. It is also the expression of a craving to experience again, as he no doubt did as a student, that ecstasy produced in the mind when language, inventing a reality on which to impose its symbols with tensions appropriate to art with no neces-sary reference to life, transcends the known facts of that experience and captures an idea which evokes a luminous comprehension without the mind being able to say what it is that it has understood, although it is certain that it has understood much more than the words it has heard.

*   *   *

The fascination with fiction common to all human beings is as enduring as the fascination of men and women with their own selves: whether we are drawn to fiction because, at the simple level, we can be comforted by the conviction that someone else's representation of people and situations and places coincides with our own view of reality; or, at a slightly higher level, where the fiction goes a little beyond its subject-matter and conveys a few ideas, because we are seeking an expression of those explanations which we have already formed, but only vaguely; or, at that level where literary language has created a fiction which we call art, because we want more than simply to relate to another being's world, more than to be given an interesting and a seemingly plausible explanation: we want, seek, and discover in art that elusive sensation given the miserable word *vision.*

If Hamlet really only wanted the play to prove his uncle's guilt, then all he needed was something at the popular level, a play the action of which would be understood by all. But either the court at Elsinore has been so cowed by Claudius that it dare not see what it is made to witness or it does not have the capacity to interpret fiction in terms of reality: for the truth is that the only person to understand the play (apart from Horatio who, however, has been coached in advance by Hamlet) has been Claudius, and language has once again failed to convey the meaning expected of it; or, Hamlet, driven to excess by his own desire to hear the language of art and have the play serve the double function of proving the King's guilt and providing an ecstasy to Hamlet's own imagination, has put on a play at his own level, that of a poet, but his audience has consisted of people familiar only with the lesser levels of art. Had everyone else seen the truth, Hamlet would have needed only to appeal to the court and won his case and got rid of Claudius without the need of personally having to murder him. He has uttered a language through the play but his audience has only heard words and that, too, without seeing a relation between the words and reality. Hamlet has seen more than the King's guilt, he has seen the failure of language. And once again: here is language and there is the world, but if there is a connection between the two, it is only in the mind of the creator of those words. His vision is intense and his despair is that he is the lone witness of the vision, condemned all his life to see it and to translate it into language which his immediate contemporaries do not understand; if the creator is a writer, like Beckett, say, he can isolate himself in strict privacy (and remain in it even when his later contemporaries begin to have the illusion that they understand his language); but a Hamlet is burdened with obligations of time and place. He is the supreme misfit. Devoted to ideas, he has to spend his time practising fencing.

*   *   *

The speech which Hamlet wants the Player to recite begins, as Hamlet himself remembers (and proceeds compulsively to declaim its first thirteen lines):

> The rugged Pyrrhus, he whose sable arms,
> Black as his purpose, did the night resemble
> When he lay couchèd in the ominous horse,
> Hath now this dread and black complexion smeared
> With heraldry more dismal.

Here is a refined literary language, entirely artificial in its assembling of phrases to insinuate a dominant image into the mind of the audience: *sable, black, night, ominous, dread, black,* and *dismal* are a constellation of words belonging to the idea of darkness. It is a self-sufficient world which resembles reality in having objects and at the same time a context of abstraction. The inevitability, or the impression in the audience's mind of truth, comes not from the relationship of these words with the reality that we know but from a conviction engendered by the vocabulary, the grammar and the general figure of speech holding the words together in one's imagination: here, the guarantee of truth is contained in the words themselves, in their apparently accurate relationship with each other. We do not need to know anything outside the passage itself to believe what we are being told, for the language which suggests its ideas as *conclusions* does so by first making us believe that it is clearly declaring, within the entire verbal formula, the *premises* on which those conclusions are founded. The entire thing is nothing but an impression in our minds; it could be a sequence of propositions of Euclidean geometry where our impression of understanding would be influenced by our acceptance of certain axioms. Literary language can be, and often is, a self-contained structure: once the poet has committed himself to some such statement as 'Shall I compare thee to a summer's day?' the rest of the sonnet is obliged to investigate ideas of time and mortality just as Euclid, once he has committed himself to the principle of the straight line cannot create a geometry dependent on wavy lines that snake about the universe. While at the literal level the Players offer Hamlet a chance to test his own hypothesis of the King's guilt, he is nevertheless thrilled, so as to speak, by the structure of straight lines which grow out of each other to form an interesting pattern because in that pattern the truth is undeniable, possessing an internal logic quite independent of what might happen in one's own daily existence.

And when the Players have gone, Hamlet is over-whelmed.

> Is it not monstrous that this player here,
> But in a fiction, in a dream of passion,
> Could force his soul so to his own conceit
> That from her working all his visage wanned,
> Tears in his eyes, distraction in his aspect,
> A broken voice, and his whole function suiting
> With forms to his conceit? And all for nothing!

'But in a fiction, in a dream of passion' reminds one of Hamlet's answer to the Queen in Act I, scene ii:

> ... all forms, moods, shapes of grief,
> That can denote me truly. These indeed seem,
> For they are actions that a man might play,

For a moment, Hamlet is led to express the belief common to human conceit that if a writer could only make one's own real passion his subject-matter then his fiction would 'drown the stage with tears' but by the end of the soliloquy he settles for what effect mere art might have 'to catch the conscience of the king'. He appreciates the strength of language as metaphor; the subject-matter of one's own life, however strong, can never match the force of literary invention: to approach a truth concerning human exist-ence, the best medium is that special type of language which is not concerned with existing humans, but which, drawing its imagery from life, assembles those universals which are descriptive of the human race. As does the play *Hamlet*.

*   *   *

KING: And can you by no drift of conference
Get from him why he puts on this confusion,
Grating so harshly all his days of quiet
With turbulent and dangerous lunacy?

Can you not, by speaking to him, get him to unfold himself? The function of the spies (Reynaldo and Rosencrantz and Guildenstern) is to establish another approach in order to discover what someone really is and the method of the spies is prescribed as an artful and deceptive use of language: Reynaldo must put 'forgeries' upon Laertes, and Rosencrantz and Guildenstern must employ a 'drift of conference'. The prescription comes from Polonius and from Claudius, the two shrewdest manipulators of language in the court.

We never hear what came of Reynaldo's mission, but it is interesting to observe that Hamlet matches Claudius's spying upon him by himself arranging the play at which he and Horatio will spy on Claudius; and he will match what Claudius has called a 'drift of conference' with an even more elaborately deceptive employment of language – the seemingly irrelevant speeches of the play. And just as Claudius has hoped that Hamlet will tell the truth about himself to Rosencrantz and Guildenstern, so Hamlet believes that 'murder, though it have no tongue, will speak' when confronted by a literary representation of its own guilt.

Claudius finds 'much content' on hearing that Hamlet is disposed to being entertained by the Players. Both to him and to the Queen, the play represents the idea of mere *play*, or pastime, something to take one's mind away from one's own problems: the language of fiction will have a diverting effect and might well be the tonic to relieve the oppression suffered by a melancholy mind; while to

Hamlet the play is to serve another function, that of carrying on an experiment with language to see if a fictive representation of reality might not precisely be the verbal formula of an undeniable truth. Two languages come together in the idea of the play: that of make-believe, as observed by that part of the audience seeking diversion, and that which is the source of belief, as observed by Hamlet; and since these two languages are actually one language, the one which everyone hears, this one language is therefore a metaphor which is susceptible to varied interpretation: to some it is purely an invention which can have no meaning unless related to an already known world; to others, those with the sensibility of a Hamlet, no world can be known unless the language is first posited, and to these it is reality which must always remain an invention made possible by the rigidly logical structure of language: a reality made accessible and then believable by one making up a fiction, one who has never suggested he was doing anything other than telling a story, a lie.

Polonius and the King are to observe the contrived meeting between Hamlet and Ophelia. She is instructed to 'Read on this book' – Polonius thus hitting upon the correct strategy to draw Hamlet. Claudius, suddenly touched in his conscience by Polonius's reference to 'devotion's visage', is led to draw a graphic image in a confessional aside:

> The harlot's cheek, beautied with plast'ring art,
> Is not more ugly to the thing that helps it
> Than is my deed to my most painted word.

One remarks upon the sequence here of *art, the thing, deed*, and *painted word*. There at the centre one has

thing / deed

flanked by

        art   *word*

especially that word which is *painted* and, therefore, nearly a synonym for *art*. Here is a nice reversal: just as Hamlet hopes that the play with its art (or, that language which blatantly is not true) will reveal a truth, so Claudius wants his language to be so full of art that no one will observe that it is masking a lie. Claudius is, in a sense, Hamlet's anti-self, his nature being pragmatic where Hamlet is given to abstraction; villain though he is, Claudius is always interesting while Hamlet, for all his virtue, is sometimes an utter bore; Claudius is a manipulator of the world around him, he is an artist among politicians, while Hamlet is rarely more than a naive metaphysician or a mediocre poet. As in his most famous soliloquy – 'To be, or not to be', a piece of writing which has had the misfortune to be so eminently quotable that one hears it from the mouths of people who have never seen or read the play and who, often, know no other line from Shakespeare, to say nothing of the generations of school children who have substituted for the *be* a four-letter word, insisting that *that* is the real question, drawing guffaws of laughter. A language which can be so easily parodied (as was *Prufrock* by its earlier readers; as, indeed, the closing lines of *The Waste Land* were by James Joyce – 'Shan't we, shan't we, shan't we'!) is always in the danger of being misunderstood; or, to put it differently, people tend to parody that which they do not understand, for laughter relieves us of tension and involving us in a camaraderie of like minds provides us with the happy illusion that we are sane and intelligent, unlike the creator of the language which we have parodied. Not only the common vulgarisation of the famous soliloquy but also interpretations based on 'action' and the characters' 'motivation' have made its simple language seem awfully portentous.

It is straining credibility if we take the soliloquy literally. If Hamlet were really contemplating suicide, then he would be a greater bore than one had feared; but clearly, Hamlet does not have the egocentricity of one who is potentially a suicide: he dwells not so much on himself as on the world, the problems which concern his own life certainly torment him but do not absorb him entirely for the problem of existence is a greater torment. Surely, he is not so cut off from life as to have no pressing anxieties, and one need not draw up a list – his father's death, his mother's behaviour, his love for Ophelia, the threat to his own life – to emphasise the point that a good many facts of his life are of a bewildering complexity; but their nature is not that which induces people to commit suicide and Hamlet has no reason to do with his immediate reality to be contemplating suicide. His formulation, 'To be, or not to be', is the phrasing of an idea which needs to be tested; it is the logical continuation of the idea which began with the 'unweeded garden'; all that is going on is that his mind is continuing to debate the imponderables: only, the debate has become heightened by the poignancy of what is going on in his own life although as far as his *existence* is concerned not even the Ghost's appearance has changed anything.

It is doubtful if the sharp-witted Prince of Denmark ever suffered from 'the proud man's contumely' (being 'very proud' himself, as he presently says to Ophelia and being highly gifted in the utterance of contumely, as when he attacks his mother); it is doubtful, too, if he had any legal suit pending or ever had to put up with 'the insolence of office' or if he truly felt that his 'patient merit' was not rewarded; and surely the Prince would be the last person in the state of Denmark 'To grunt and sweat under a weary life'. Perhaps the 'oppressor's wrong' and the 'pangs of despised love' can be said to refer to his own experience, but much of his speech is impersonal and generalised, composed of propositions with which to pursue an intellectual enquiry. Such language as 'the whips and scorns of time', 'Th' oppressor's wrong' and 'the law's delay' belongs to an essay an English earl might write for the *New Statesman* and is hardly the phraseology of a suicide note. A person does not commit suicide because there are six or seven generalisations about the oppressed human situation on his mind.

Hamlet is not contemplating suicide but testing the meaning of life by positing its very opposite, and in his conclusions he is very much like a Beckett character who knowing that life is meaningless realises that death will not solve anything, for it will not guarantee the elusive meaning but either prolong the anguish in the after-life ('the dread of something after death . . . puzzles the will') or, if there is no after-life, make the one life even more absurdly meaningless. And like many of Beckett's characters, Hamlet is obliged to pass the time by talking to himself, now testing one hypothesis and now another. (Cf. Beckett in *The Unnamable*: 'But say I succeed in dying, to adopt the most comfortable hypothesis, without having been able to believe I ever lived, I know to my cost it is not that they wish for me. For it has happened to me many times already, without their having granted me as much as a brief sick-leave among the worms, before resurrecting me. But who knows, this time, what the future holds in store.')

The 'pale cast of thought' makes action futile, especially the one action which is the extremest of all – self-murder. And yet the mind must compulsively go on combining words, the ceaseless flow of language cannot be checked in whatever time or place the body dwells, and besides there is always the possibility that the next new combination of words might be the formula of revelation.

The encounter with Ophelia follows. Hamlet, who has been weighing propositions in his mind, his abstract introspection happening in a generalised language, suddenly tears into Ophelia with some of his most devastatingly scholarly language, so that he has hardly begun when the poor girl, sensing the confusion in her own mind, cries out:

What means your lordship?

She has already made her little token speech, a pretty little poetic gesture that a refined young lady might learn the formula of at a finishing school:

My honoured lord, you know right well you did,
And with them words of so sweet breath composed
As made these things more rich. Their perfume lost,
Take these again, for to the noble mind
Rich gifts wax poor when givers prove unkind.

That ought to have been enough to make the man she believes is in love with her to enfold her in his arms, but Hamlet does not even appear to listen to her and a moment later he launches his tirade.

Ay, truly; for the power of beauty will sooner transform honesty from what it is to a bawd than the force of honesty can translate beauty into his likeness. This was sometime a paradox, but now the time gives it proof.

She is dumbfounded, and he adds: 'I did love you once.' At last a sentence she can understand and respond to: 'Indeed, my lord, you made me believe so.' But Hamlet goes on:

You should not have believed me, for virtue cannot so inoculate our old stock but we shall relish of it.

Again she is speechless and Hamlet adds a simpler statement: 'I loved you not', completing a neat paradox. 'I was the more deceived', she wails self-pityingly. Hamlet's speeches to her become violent and are rapidly spoken (the preponderance of monosyllables – 'be thou as chaste as ice, as pure as snow' – demands a fast, agitated speech from the actor); they contain ambiguous ideas which are probably beyond Ophelia's comprehension. She can answer only when he adds a simple statement when the main torrent of his ideas has passed – i.e. 'Where's your father?'

Ophelia can speak at her own pace again only when he has abandoned her:

> O what a noble mind is here o'erthrown!
> The courtier's, soldier's, scholar's eye, tongue, sword,
> Th' expectancy and rose of the fair state,
> The glass of fashion, and the mould of form,
> The observed of all observers, quite, quite down!

Typically, like all simple people whose understanding of language is at the level of mundane reality and who can rarely see beyond the narrow world of their own self (Ophelia: 'And I, of ladies most deject and wretched'), her response to Hamlet's complexity of language is to believe that he must be mad.

(The earlier readers of 'Prufrock' believed the poem to be 'absolutely insane' – the phrase is Harold Monro's; scientists whose discoveries challenge existing beliefs are considered to be people of questionable sanity and the phrase 'mad scientist' is in common usage; and a country like Soviet Russia, threatened by the language of its dissidents, puts them into psychiatric wards.)

Hamlet has attacked Ophelia for the sexuality, or the principle of procreation, which her womanhood represents.

His violent speeches to her are not an attempt to prove his madness to anyone who might be overhearing him. He has been thinking of life and death: death, he has concluded, is no resolution and then says to Ophelia, 'it were better my mother had not borne me'. (Cf. Beckett's Molloy, who remarks of his mother: '. . . her who brought me into the world, through the hole in her arse if my memory is correct. First taste of the shit.' Hamlet's violence has become Molloy's obscenity, Hamlet's hatred of life Molloy's disgust with birth.) And here is the fair Ophelia, containing within her the awful potential for creating life and, what is worse, his own desire for her makes him an accomplice. In his present mood, he, who believes that his own conception was an appalling act, turns away with revulsion ('No, not I . . .') on hearing Ophelia say

> My lord, I have remembrances of yours
> That I have longèd long to redeliver.

For, in the sexual act, too, he would give her that which she would redeliver. What follows is not madness but a rage against life.

Only the King, perceiving that Hamlet's language 'was not like madness', comes closest to understanding the abstract nature of Hamlet's torment:

> Love? His affections do not that way tend,
> Nor what he spake, though it lacked form a little,
> Was not like madness. There's something in his soul
> O'er which his melancholy sits on brood . . .

Being burdened by his own guilt, however, Claudius is obliged to translate his own ignorance of what it is in Hamlet's soul into a potential threat. He had better not take any chances. Hamlet must away to England. It is a perfectly wise move, for this kind of Hamlet is a threat not only to the King but also to the state: the poet must be banished, the dissident put away; and the appearance of doing the right thing for the security of the state will camouflage his own need to eliminate Hamlet.

But Polonius, despairing at losing the Prince as a potential son-in-law, comes up with a stratagem – let the Queen meet Hamlet in private and ask him to tell the truth, with Polonius himself listening from a concealed position.

Everyone is anxious to hear the meaning which each is convinced is surely there: Polonius that Hamlet loves Ophelia, the King that Hamlet suspects him of killing his brother, and Hamlet is looking at the idea of meaning itself. While there is dramatic conflict in the play at the level of human action, there is this more complex conflict at the level of human thought.

HAMLET: Speak the speech, I pray you, as I pronounced it to you, trippingly on the tongue.

This is one occasion when Hamlet can tell another to speak in such a way that he, Hamlet, can hear precisely what he wants to hear down to the subtlest gesture and the most distant of nuances. If only the exhortation to *speak* made by everyone from Francisco to Claudius could elicit a similarly rehearsed response! All problems of the relationship between language and reality would vanish then, for we, commanding the speech we wish to hear, would then be the creators of reality.

(Cf. Wallace Stevens, especially in *The Idea of Order at Key West*:

> It was her voice that made
> The sky acutest at its vanishing.
> She measured to the hour its solitude.
> She was the single artificer of the world
> In which she sang. And when she sang, the sea,
> Whatever self it had, became the self
> That was her song.

And in *The Man With the Blue Guitar* in which 'The thinking of art seems final when / The thinking of god is smoky dew.')

Hamlet's instructions to the Players are not merely Shakespeare's attempt to lay down some basic principles of acting but they contain an experiment of Hamlet's to see if unreality cannot be made to assume the characteristics of reality to such a degree that it has the very appearance of reality so that he can observe if this reality, made to the special order of a human will and bounded so neatly by time and place that it can be comprehended fully, cannot offer that vision which ordinary existence has so far failed to give him. Hamlet can be dismissive of ordinary people, 'the groundlings, who for the most part are capable of nothing but inexplicable dumb shows and noise'. He has the intellectual's, and the artist's, contempt for ordinary people who are content with surfaces; but 'inexplicable dumb shows' are also to be despised because they are inexplicable and *dumb*, which is to say they do not serve the command *Stand and unfold yourself*, for they do not *speak*.

Hamlet's main stricture, of course, is that the actors should be natural: 'Suit the action to the word, the word to the action, with this special observance, that you o'erstep not the modesty of nature.' The play he wants to see has to be so lifelike that it is reality itself. His intention to devise a play in which he can catch the conscience of the King has already exceeded itself and become an enterprise calculated to test reality itself. But when performed, the play provides him with nothing other than circumstantial proof of the King's guilt, though seeing art achieve that effect briefly produces in Hamlet a crazed excitement.

(The dialogue between the Player King and Player Queen is so boring that, were it not for his soliloquy which soon follows, one would think Claudius had walked out like some modern critics at a new play, impatient with trite dialogue. One does wonder, though, why Claudius who has been so cunning in manipulating the court simply did not sit it out, pretending that he was having a great time. But, of course, there's so much a writer can do to make his characters consistent. And incidentally, I have never seen a production of *Hamlet* which has contained the entire play within the play; most producers have used only the dumb show – which makes a nice comment on modern audiences, reducing us all to groundlings!)

Hamlet is so exhilarated by the apparent success of the aborted play in proving the King's guilt that he breaks out into verses (much as Ophelia does later when she goes mad) and calls for music – that purest of expressions to whose condition (the tag from Walter Pater has been quoted so often it has become a cliché) all art aspires. Art has succeeded, at least partially, in having shown Hamlet what he wanted to see and the best gratitude that can be expressed to it is to listen to its most abstract formulation – just as one whose prayers have been answered, saving him from an illness, will not embark at once upon any form of self-indulgence but will devote himself to the reading of a holy book to prove the continuing sincerity of his devotions and to experience a purer level of religious ecstasy, for now that the problem has been solved there can be no ulterior motive in the action, only the desire to experience the thing for itself. But Hamlet is not allowed such a satisfaction, for first Rosencrantz and Guildenstern return demanding that he put his 'discourse into some frame' and obliging him to 'make a wholesome answer', and then Polonius comes back to say solemnly and without his usual convoluted phraseology that 'the Queen would speak' with him. Yet once more, the instructions which come from the world outside the self are that one find a proper form for one's language and that one use words which are understandable. Rosencrantz says quite simply:

'She desires to speak with you in her closet ere you go to bed.'

There is little reason for the scene to be prolonged another sixty or so lines but Hamlet, having just experienced the ecstasy of what artistic language can achieve, is being drawn back to the ordinary use of words, which activity all his earlier experience has taught him leads nowhere; and so, instinctively, he takes a recorder from the Players when Guildenstern makes a hypocritical statement about his love for him and says, 'I do not well understand that.' And then immediately asks, 'Will you play upon this pipe?' – this pipe, this instrument, within which are contained all combinations of musical phrases, but Guildenstern can do nothing with it, no more than a foreigner with a language he does not know but who is given a dictionary of it and asked to make combinations of words in such a way that they add to a poem. It is in utter frustration that Guildenstern replies, 'But these cannot I command to any utt'rance of harmony; I have not the skill'.

Hamlet can then abuse him and Rosencrantz – 'there is much music, excellent voice, in this little organ, yet cannot you make it speak' – for their presumption that they can play on him, make him *speak*. At one level, he is satisfying, in a petty way, a craving for revenge, but at another, it is significant that the example he has chosen to make his point is to do with creating meaningful sound out of an object which in itself is inert and silent, like the human tongue, and that the entire thrust of the scene is to counterpoint the original 'Nay, answer me' with 'yet cannot you make it speak'. There follows the little exchange with Polonius concerning the cloud.

HAMLET: Do you see yonder cloud that's almost in the shape of a camel?

POLONIUS : By th' mass and 'tis, like a camel indeed.
HAMLET : Methinks it is like a weasel.
POLONIUS : It is backed like a weasel.
HAMLET : Or like a whale.
POLONIUS : Very like a whale.

Polonius is remarkably submissive and disinclined to argue in this exchange, but he is the only person in the play who is likely to understand that Hamlet's point is not merely to assert himself but that what Hamlet is suggesting is something that he, Polonius, cannot deny: it is to do with the arbitrariness of words, for here 'camel', 'weasel' and 'whale' are words which do not refer to the class of things we define as camels, weasels and whales, but are *merely* words that signify nothing but appearances or only their own sounds. Also, the three sounds could be like the sounds made on a recorder by one who does not know how to play it but, idly picking up the pipe, blows upon it, without harmony. *Peep, peep, peep*; or perhaps *peep, poop, pip*; or perhaps, if the instrument is the human tongue, *camel, weasel, whale.*

It could also be, of course, an attempt to demonstrate his continuing madness and Polonius's quiet acquiescence could be the delicate manner of one not wanting to aggravate another's disturbed mental state; but the imagery, and the form in which Hamlet puts it, does indicate that even when he is most profoundly engaged in attending to the problems of guilt and retribution his mind cannot avoid testing correspondences between words and the reality they represent. To have acquired certainty of Claudius's guilt is a minor victory; the real prize would be to have certainty of knowledge.

*   *   *

Wittgenstein: 'Isn't the question "Have these words a meaning?" similar to "Is that a tool?" asked as one produces, say, a hammer? I say "Yes, it's a hammer". But what if the thing that any of us would take for a hammer were somewhere else a missile, for example, or a conductor's baton? Now make the application yourself.'

CLOUD – *camel, weasel, whale.*

*   *   *

Having received Polonius's acquiescence that so formless a thing as a cloud can contain the idea of things which we think we know (thus reaching an epistemological dead-end, for the words no longer refer to objects and are only themselves, and therefore without meaning; and the sequence need not end with 'whale' – it could continue endlessly and contain the variations of other poets, such as Wallace Stevens's

> Let be be finale of seem.
> The only emperor is the emperor of ice-cream.

For it is all, to use another phrase of Stevens, 'clouds as jugglery'), Hamlet can then, satisfied that this enquiry into language can give him nothing, return to his mundane reality and attend to his mother. But what will he do on seeing her?

> I will speak daggers to her, but use none.
> My tongue and soul in this be hypocrites:
> How in my words somever she be shent,
> To give them seals never, my soul, consent!

Speak; *words*. He can never escape from language.

The King, who had been the first to perceive that 'what he spake . . . / Was not like madness', now says of Hamlet

> I like him not, nor stands it safe with us
> To let his madness range.

The play just abandoned, his own guilt nearly made public, Claudius desperately needs everyone to believe what he himself knows to be false. These are the first words we hear from him since he walked out of the play and one observes how he has summoned all his resources of state-craft, one of which is his cunning manipulation of language, and in this sentence where the greatest stress falls on the syllable *mad* the speech is calculated to presume and strengthen a conviction in others and by implication explain what has happened and make necessary what he is about to suggest.

Left alone, the King broods upon his guilt, wondering how a formula of language could serve as sufficient prayer.

> But, O, what form of prayer
> Can serve my turn? 'Forgive me my foul murder'?

Only in heaven 'the action lies / In his true nature' but in 'the corrupted currents of this world' we may continue to deceive; for here, we are attached to things ('My crown, mine own ambition, and my queen') and our language cannot separate us from these things: whereas prayer articulates itself as an abstraction, and however pure a form it takes it can have no meaning as long as we are obliged to turn from it to a world of things. Prayer cannot help Claudius, not only because his repentence is insincere as long as he keeps 'those effects' for which he committed the murder but also because of the idea that if the language of things can be used to deceive then what certainty is there that the language of heaven is always true?

> My words fly up, my thoughts remain below.
> Words without thoughts never to heaven go.

Words are forever detaching themselves from ideas, and human thoughts can never become the pure forms of heaven no matter what intensity of transcendental effort we exercise.

While the King is at prayer, Hamlet, on his way to his mother, sees him, realises he has a chance to revenge his father, but says 'That would be scanned', meaning that he should look into his proposition, and proceeds to make an investigation of logic in order to understand the word 'revenge':

> A villain kills my father, and for that
> I, his sole son, do this same villain send
> To heaven.
> Why, this is hire and salary, not revenge.

It sounds like a student's first exercises in syllogism. It is not revenge because it does not guarantee the uncle will go to hell; also, the reality does not conform to the propositions

in his mind and Hamlet gets carried away inventing the
reality he would prefer – which invention, characteristi-
cally, is a literary structure:

> When he is drunk asleep, or in his rage,
> Or in th' incestuous pleasure of his bed,
> At game a-swearing, or about some act
> That has no relish of salvation in't –
> Then trip him, that his heels may kick at heaven,
> And that his soul may be as damned and black
> As hell, whereto it goes.

The language of his imagination is richer than the logic
with which he has just tried to analyse the immediate
situation; certainly, the poetic image in his mind of
Claudius kicking his heels at heaven is more interesting to
him than what he would see if he now stabbed Claudius
in the back – in which case all he would see would be a
dead body. In the alternative which he projects, he is not
responsible to facts but, like a poet, takes delight in the
invention of imagery to pursue a private vision, thus re-
lieving himself from the obligation to participate in his
immediate reality. It is not procrastination; the immediate
reality is not exciting enough for him to perform what has
to be an extraordinary deed – he is quite capable of action
but, as with the pirates on the high seas and as with the
duel with Laertes, Hamlet needs a poetic or a dramatic
setting: if there has to be action, it must be carried out
under the illusion of significance or for that extreme
reason, survival.

*   *   *

Polonius, coming to inform the Queen that Hamlet is on
his way, says, just before he withdraws to eavesdrop, 'I'll

silence me even here.' It is a perfect statement to make for one who has spoken so many words and, of course, Polonius is in position to perceive the poignant irony which he has unwittingly uttered.

And a moment later the dialogue begins between mother and son:

QUEEN: Come, come you answer with an idle tongue.
HAMLET: Go, go, you question with a wicked tongue.

The dialogue is at once about the *kind of language* one may use; the Queen has been instructed to 'be round with him' and Hamlet is determined to 'speak daggers to her'. It is immediately apparent even to her that in any dialogue he is going to outwit her, for she simply does not have the resources of language to be able to talk to him, so that within ten lines she nearly abandons the attempt, saying, 'Nay, then I'll set those to you that can speak.' For the purpose of Hamlet's visit is that he unfold himself and if she cannot speak the words necessary to achieve that result, then someone else will, someone who *can speak*. The vehement note in Hamlet's speech makes her panic, and a moment later Polonius is killed, Hamlet no doubt hoping that it is Claudius who is hiding behind the curtain, for that would fulfil his recent fantasy of killing Claudius when he is doing something demonstrably immoral. It is interesting to note in passing that his victim is unseen – it is an *abstract* murder, almost as if Hamlet were killing an idea for which rational words had failed him. The action of killing a human being seems to have no effect upon him at all, he might as well have swatted a fly; his mind is entirely upon what he has to *speak* to his mother, and if his emotions are overwrought, it is because he has to use a language so violent that when he does so, she cries out:

What have I done that thou dar'st wag thy tongue
In noise so rude against me?

His answer is an aggressively eloquent flow of speech, the
words unfolding her self to the Queen so that she pleads

> O Hamlet, speak no more.
> Thou turn'st mine eyes into my very soul . . .

But Hamlet will not stop now that words appear to be
revealing truth, and the Queen cries desperately

> O, speak to me no more.
> These words like daggers enter in my ears.
> No more, sweet Hamlet.

Still he hurls the words at her and still she cries, 'No more.'
And then: '*Enter* GHOST.' She is saved. The words which
were holding a mirror up to her, making her begin to see
'black and grainèd spots' in her soul, can now be rejected
as having no meaning, for it is with great relief that she
says, seeing Hamlet talk to the Ghost, 'Alas, he's mad'.
The Ghost's appearance has the effect of terminating
Hamlet's verbal violence and making him adopt a softer
tone when, following the Ghost's last words, 'Speak to her,
Hamlet', he changes his language from being abusive to
one which shows a solicitous concern, so that the Queen is
more inclined to be understanding.

Hamlet may well suffer from the Oedipus Complex and
his statement to his mother – 'go not to my uncle's bed' –
could be quoted to support that thesis. But as we observed
in the scene with Ophelia, Hamlet has a horror of procreation – 'it were better my mother had not borne me':
now he pleads with his mother to refrain from sex; not

necessarily because of some buried guilt, some suppressed fantasy in which he has slept with his mother or desired her sexually, but possibly because the event of the mother being penetrated is a *repetition* of the very event that led to his own conception. In the mind of one who finds worthless all the uses of this world, to whom the world is an unweeded garden and existence without meaning, that one event is charged with so much disgust that it has assumed the texture of evil.

*   *   *

KING: There's matter in these sighs. These profound heaves
You must translate; 'tis fit we understand them.

From *Nay, answer me* (Act I, scene i) to *You must translate* (Act IV, scene i) the vocabulary has changed but the speaker is making much the same demand. The language we hear, or the signs we observe, need to be translated and what we believe to be meaning, or truth, is often no more than a conviction that we have understood, which is to say that the speech we have heard is translated, or interpreted, in the mind according to a formula already embedded there. But while the French word *l'eau* might become *water* in the mind of an Englishman who knows French, or *low* in the mind of one who does not, a shimmering on the horizon can also become *water* in the mind of one crossing a desert: the idea into which a word, or an image, is translated depends on factors quite independent of, and sometimes entirely irrelevant to, that word. When we use language, our presumption is that our correspondent has eaten the same excellent dinner that we have and that he is not likely to mistake our description of snow for the icing on a cake. And, of course, frequently we are obliged to confess to incomprehension and to say: *You must translate.*

When the Queen does translate, she does so in a manner calculated to convince Claudius of his own preconception, for the first word she uses in her explanation is 'Mad'. She has learned to speak in Claudius's own cunning manner.

> Mad as the sea and wind when both contend

she says of Hamlet, choosing a figure of speech which can accommodate the word 'mad' without her actually needing to say that Hamlet is mad, for the 'mad', in her context, can mean 'enraged'. It is her most subtle speech in the play; she who has wanted 'more matter, with less art', is here herself artful, wanting to disguise from Claudius the true nature of her meeting with Hamlet; and she succeeds in creating a misleading impression without having told a lie. Reynaldo could not have done better.

Claudius instructs Rosencrantz and Guildenstern to find Hamlet and tells them to 'speak fair' to him while he himself, with the Queen, will 'call up our wisest friends / And let them know . . .' Meanings are to be divulged, but there is no guarantee that after hearing them anyone will *know*.

Hamlet no longer needs to feign madness but appears madder than ever, mocking Rosencrantz and Guildenstern with insults (and it is Rosencrantz who now does the real feigning, saying, 'I understand you not, my lord' when there is little not to understand and surely he has enough experience of figures of speech to comprehend the trite image 'sponge') and running away from them when they are about to take him to the King. It is now important to the King, and therefore to those serving him, to continue to believe that Hamlet is mad. Claudius says, 'How dangerous it is that this man goes loose!' not because Hamlet is a lunatic murderer at large who might strike another innocent victim but because Hamlet has revealed that he knows Claudius's guilty secret: and that line of Claudius's is yet another example of how his language is invariably charged with cunning. And when he adds a moment later

> To bear all smooth and even,
> This sudden sending him away must seem
> Deliberate pause.

Claudius is proclaiming himself the creator of appearances which mankind believes to be reality. While to Hamlet the uses of this world are worthless because they do not show him *the world*, Claudius is of that world of which he himself manipulates the uses. And when Hamlet is finally brought to him in Act IV, scene iii, there is genuine bewilderment in the King's 'What dost thou mean by this?' Perhaps he is only provoking Hamlet to utter complicated speech which will be seen as a lunatic's ravings by the witnesses present, but for a moment he does appear entirely confused, and the question, 'What dost thou mean by this?' is profounder than at first appears, demanding rational explanation while wanting evidence of irrationality and at the same time being expressed in the anguished tone of someone who finds meaninglessness an unbearable pain. When Hamlet's answer is in the simple 'Nothing but . . .' formula, Claudius immediately reverts to his earlier question and changes his tone to that of one determined to have the business done with at once: 'Where is Polonius?' And most businesslike, he resolves the matter of finding Polonius's body and despatching Hamlet off to England in a dozen lines.

Act IV, scene iv: '*A Plain in Denmark*'. And this is where Hamlet, enquiring of Fortinbras's Captain the nature of the army's engagement, is informed

> Truly to speak, and with no addition,
> We go to gain a little patch of ground
> That hath in it no profit but the name.
> To pay five ducats, five, I would not farm it,
> Nor will it yield to Norway or the Pole
> A ranker rate, should it be sold in fee.

Truly to speak. Here is one, an anonymous soldier, telling Hamlet the truth. All the warlike preparations, all this martial show; and all for a worthless *little patch of ground*. The actions of both the Poles, in defending it, and the Norwegians, in invading it, are meaningless and yet both parties are prepared to die for it; here is a representation of humanity which does not pause to consider the absolute futility of its actions but goes about asserting the belief that what it does is *right*, thus substituting the fact of an unbearable existence with a stimulating morality: when reality fails us, an abstract language gives us a reason to be. It is the delicate hypocrisy of religions which knowing that we can never see offer us visions; and it is our subtle delusion that since we cannot see, therefore there must be visions available to us. Our vanity will not put up with a little patch of ground.

*   *   *

We go to gain a little patch of ground . . . In Patrick White's novel, *Voss*, the explorer Voss leads a party of men into the interior of Australia but he is neither a scientist nor, like Fortinbras, a soldier. Seeker after self-dissolution and some elusive mystical revelation, he has left the forests of his native Germany to surrender his body to the desert of Australia, equating physical agony with spiritual ecstasy, but all one observes is the mutilation of flesh and a brain fever. The people with him have somehow failed in the physical world, each is possessed by an inner desperation but no one can find the words which will release him from torment. They can reach nowhere:

> They were riding eternally over the humped and hateful earth, which the sun had seared until the spent and crumbly stuff was become highly treacherous. It was, indeed, the bare crust of the earth. . . . The ghosts of things haunted here, and in that early light the men and animals which had arrived were but adding to the ghost-life of the place.

Some deliberately seek the little patch or *the bare crust of the earth* where the material world has become a ghost to see what the spirit will not discover, and others, like Beckett's Molloy, find themselves there:

> But it is not the kind of place where you go, but where you find yourself, sometimes, not knowing how, and

which you cannot leave at will, and where you find yourself without any pleasure, but with more perhaps than in those places you can escape from, by making an effort, places full of mystery, full of the familiar mysteries. I listen and the voice is of a world collapsing endlessly, a frozen world, under a faint untroubled sky, enough to see by, yes, and frozen too. And I hear it murmur that all wilts and yields, as if loaded down, but here there are no loads, and the ground too, unfit for loads, and the light too, down towards an end it seems can never come. For what possible end to these wastes where true light never was, nor any upright thing, nor any true foundation, but only these leaning things, forever lapsing and crumbling away, beneath a sky without memory of morning or hope of night.

Cf. Hart Crane in *North Labrador*:

> A land of leaning ice
> Hugged by plaster-grey arches of sky,
> Flings itself silently
> Into eternity.

Where the poet desperately uses words, demanding meaning, but

> Cold-hushed, there is only the shifting of moments
> That journey toward no Spring –
> No birth, no death, no time nor sun
> In answer.

Or T. S. Eliot in 'Burnt Norton':

Here is a place of disaffection
Time before and time after
In a dim light: neither daylight
Investing form with lucid stillness
Turning shadow into transient beauty
With slow rotation suggesting permanence
Nor darkness to purify the soul
Emptying the sensual with deprivation
Cleansing affection from the temporal.
Neither plenitude nor vacancy. Only a flicker
Over the strained time-ridden faces...

Or William Carlos Williams in *To Elsie*:

as if the earth under our feet
were
an excrement of some sky

and we degraded prisoners
destined
to hunger until we eat filth

while the imagination strains
after deer
going by fields of goldenrod...

Always, the imagination strains, putting words together to see if the idea in the mind takes the shape of meaning, pondering propositions to see if the next one in the series – so compelling is the illusion of logic – will not contain the elusive truth, always the refusal to accept the visible fact of the bare crust of the earth, an excrement of some sky, the little patch of ground where there is neither plenitude nor vacancy, and no answer.

It has been stated that *Hamlet* is the objective correlative of literature; that is perhaps a sensational way of saying that a substantial body of literature has sought a new imagery to investigate the very idea that Hamlet's mind has not been able to articulate.

* * *

Hamlet's soliloquy which follows the statement about the little patch of ground shows him at first to be chastising himself for having delayed the revenge. But the *occasions* which *inform against* him are the visible facts of this world and his despair is that he cannot escape the trivial banality of existence, for after the opening statement, his first *thought* is one more philosophical proposition:

> What is a man,
> If his chief good and market of his time
> Be but to sleep and feed? A beast, no more.

But this, he reasons, is unacceptable:

> Sure he that made us with such large discourse,
> Looking before and after, gave us not
> That capability and godlike reason
> To fust in us unused.

Discourse, that understanding through language, and a capacity to observe cause and effect, ought to produce more tenable convictions than he has been able to arrive at; instead, he is either a beast who has no concept of responsibility or a rational creature of such complexity that he is absorbed entirely in 'Looking before and after'.

       – I do not know
Why yet I live to say, 'This thing's to do,'
Sith I have cause, and will, and strength, and means
To do't.

He is not deluding himself about his will, the statement is
a factual one; his failure comes from his desire to discover
from the rational processes within his own mind that statement which would be an absolutely irrefutable instruction
that he perform the action: he is, to use an image I once
heard from a philosopher, in the position of a centipede
which has happily crawled about the universe as long as
it has been driven by instinct but becomes totally para-
lysed as soon as it begins to think about its feet and wonders which one it ought to put forward first. Notice, too,
the irony of 'I do not know' in the last quotation, an irony
sustained by the isolated position of the phrase in the
structure of the verse where it seems to be suspended
almost outside the context. Unlike Hamlet, Fortinbras
'Makes mouths at the invisible event' and does not need
'great argument' to send twenty thousand men to their
death for no commendable reason. Fortinbras is not only
a reminder to Hamlet of what kind of a prince he himself
ought to be but also an example of a leader who invents
causes, one who uses language not to ask questions but to
give orders, who substitutes metaphysical quest with
physical conquest, who, throughout the play, seems to be
marching about the frontiers of Denmark with his feet
firmly on the ground, finally to be seen as the only one
capable of inheriting the earth – which final fact is one of
the loveliest subtleties in the play: it is Fortinbras who
goes to capture the little patch of ground and if the patch
is the play's symbol for the earth, then Fortinbras, with an

irony which he will never comprehend, fully deserves to inherit it.

Hamlet concludes the soliloquy with the resolution

> O, from this time forth,
> My thoughts be bloody, or be nothing worth!

Let language-propositions be replaced by action-propositions; but that final phrase is curious for it means more than just 'worthless'. If we see 'nothing worth' as an inversion, which it is, for the sake of the rhyme, the phrase can mean 'worthy of nothing'. All of Beckett's major characters are constantly muttering thoughts and are very much obsessed by that which is 'nothing worth' in the special sense of having to do with *Nothing*. If one could utter a proposition which showed the true worth of Nothing, we could make a great leap in this matter of language and knowledge. Hamlet's obvious intention, of course, is to say 'worthless', but he has not simply said that, and his mind even when he is determinedly trying to come to grips with a world of action cannot help uttering phrases which belong to no world outside that of Language itself. For it is not in the world of real things but in one of *nothingness* that the unobtainable vision is to be perceived: for its truth to be guaranteed, the vision must not concern itself with the unreliable and banal objects of space and time. Cf. Eliot in *The Waste Land*:

> and I knew nothing,
> Looking into the heart of light, the silence.

Ophelia has gone mad and the Queen says: 'I will not speak with her.'

One cannot speak with the mad, they talk a different language; one does not wish to hear them either, they might utter something so mad that it is a revelation of truth. And the Queen has already been battered by words, she had to beg Hamlet to *speak no more*, for she had believed him to be mad and his enraged language had suddenly revealed him as both sane and in possession of truths she had not wanted to confront, and here is Ophelia who is decidedly mad and God knows what she might not say. No. *I will not speak with her*. The Queen is terrified of words.

GENTLEMAN: She is importunate, indeed distract.

As was Hamlet in Act I when he saw his father's Ghost and called to him importunately, 'O, answer me! / Let me not burst in ignorance . . .' The Gentleman then says of Ophelia that she

                    . . . says she hears
         There's tricks i' th' world . . .

that she 'speaks things in doubt' and that

Her speech is nothing
Yet the unshapèd use of it doth move
The hearers to collection.

She whose language had no responsible relationship with reality but went about giving an impression of logical speech has now abandoned the world of appearances. Something in her mind tells her that there are tricks in the world, and these are not only deceptions which she has experienced, finding herself cheated of the happiness she had expected, but also deceptions to do with her understanding of the world itself: she has arrived at Hamlet's perception but not having Hamlet's rational language can make nothing of it: *Her speech is nothing*, her words are 'nothing worth'. And when Laertes sees her later in this scene, he says, 'This nothing's more than matter.' It is matter itself, this *Nothing*.

And when she enters, she utters a simple truth in her madness: she sings, and the imagery of her song is to do with death and procreation. That is all that vision reveals. (As with Eliot's Sweeney: 'Birth, and copulation and death. / That's all, that's all, that's all, that's all, / Birth, and copulation, and death.')

But she breaks off her song to say, 'Lord, we know what we are, but know not what we may be.' And 'Pray let's have no words of this'. She is the only one who can say with perfect conviction that *we know what we are*, but the language with which she reveals this is of 'unshapèd use': her hearers can understand her only intuitively. A paraphrase of a poem does not convey a comprehensive meaning of the poem and the meaning which we intuit is fuller, we believe, than could be obtained from a prose statement of the same idea. *Pray let's have no words of this*, let us listen to the song. The philosopher ends with silence, the poet dies singing.

HORATIO: What are they that would speak with me?
SERVANT: Seafaring men, sir. They say they have letters
for you.

It is as if another Ghost were appearing to Horatio, for
there is a suggestion about 'seafaring men' as messengers
from another world, an idea hinted at by what Horatio
goes on to say:

> I do not know from part of the world
> I should be greeted, if not from Lord Hamlet.

And when the sailors give him Hamlet's letter, Horatio
reads in it 'I have words to speak in thine ear will make
thee dumb'. We are reminded of what the Ghost had said
to Hamlet:

> I could a tale unfold whose lightest word
> Would harrow up thy soul, freeze thy young blood,
> Make thy two eyes like stars start from their spheres,
> Thy knotted and combinèd locks to part,
> And each particular hair to stand on end
> Like quills upon the fretful porpentine.

Hamlet's line is a compression of the same idea, he too has a tale to unfold; and like the Ghost, his tale will concern his own body.

*   *   *

Hamlet's return as if he were a Ghost is also suggested by the phrase 'my sudden and more strange return' in the letter he writes to the King, whose first comment on reading it is 'What should this mean?', and to whom Hamlet's return must indeed be ghostlike since he had every expectation that he would be dead by now.

What should this mean? is doubly significant, being on the literal level a perfectly natural question for the King to ask; and secondly, in terms of the play's preoccupation with language and knowledge and the attempt to arrive at that combination of words which creates a meaning which, hitting upon a correspondence between language and reality, at last breaks down the barrier between the two, the question echoes the central obsession of the play. If we could only say what *this* meant!

Much of this scene (Act IV, scene vii), however, consists of the dialogue between Claudius and Laertes in which there first is another brilliant example of the use of language to persuade, in which Claudius uses not mere suggestion, as he did in Act I, scene ii, but sound political reasoning; and second, after the letter from Hamlet has been received, the subtle use made of it by Claudius to let Laertes believe that it is his own idea to become a fellow-conspirator and to be the instrument of Hamlet's death – '. . . if you could devise it so / That I might be the organ.' Once Claudius has manœuvered Laertes to this commitment, he makes certain of Laertes's loyalty by flattering him, and it is pertinent to note that the device he uses parallels the kind of instructions which Polonius had given

Reynaldo (the lesson of 'put on him / What forgeries you please', and Claudius, indeed, uses the word 'forgery' in his speech). In order to flatter Laertes, Claudius praises a Norman visitor, using precisely the kind of language which Polonius was at pains to instruct Reynaldo to use:

> Two months since
> Here was a gentleman of Normandy.
> I have seen myself, and served against, the French,
> And they can well on horseback, but this gallant
> Had witchcraft in't. He grew unto his seat,
> And to such wondrous doing brought his horse
> As had he been incorpsed and demi-natured
> With the brave beast. So far he topped my thought
> That I, in forgery of shapes and tricks,
> Come short of what he did.

The speech is long for what it says but the calculation behind it is to create a sense of wonder, and identification, in the mind of Laertes, and no sooner has Laertes recognised the man than Claudius says:

> He made confession of you,
> And gave you such a masterly report,
> For art and exercise in your defence,
> And for your rapier most especial,
> That he cried out 'twould be a sight indeed
> If one could match you.

The technique is transparent, and if one wonders why it is drawn out at such length one answer has to be that Shakespeare is presenting a comprehensive example of the language of corruption which he had, through Polonius, earlier defined in structural outline. So carefully studied

is Claudius's technique that watching Laertes accept his
flattery as truth, he leaves him in a delicate suspense for
a moment, saying, 'Now, out of this – ', while pretending
that he is thinking to himself, so that Laertes, who by now
is totally committed to the King's cause, asks anxiously,
'What out of this, my lord?' And with greater subtlety,
Claudius, instead of answering, asks Laertes a question,
and so involves him in an abstract language to do with
parental love that when he finally asks

> Hamlet comes back; what would you undertake
> To show yourself in deed your father's son
> More than in words?

Laertes is obliged quickly to make that answer which will
most convince Claudius and which Claudius has, indeed,
put him in a corner to utter: 'To cut his throat i' th'
church!' It is a statement which even in its violent ex-
tremity has logically got to be the culminating conclusion
of all that Claudius has said.

It is a victory of the King's political shrewdness to have
converted an inflamed rebel not merely into an ally but
also into a passionately committed conspirator and his only
weapon has been a cunning language. The victory is almost
ruined by the Queen coming in to announce that Ophelia
has drowned herself and when the King says to her at the
end of the scene, 'How much I had to do to calm his rage!',
he is expressing both his fear that Laertes might again
take to rebellion and also a statement about his artful
employment of language with which he has attempted to
win over Laertes.

And in the Queen's speech describing Ophelia's drown-
ing, one remarks that what one sees is almost Prufrock's
vision, for Ophelia was 'mermaidlike' and 'she chanted

snatches of old lauds' before going to her 'muddy death'.

The mud which is all there is of the world in Beckett's *How It Is* and through which the *I* of the novel is journeying towards Pim:

> on my face in the mud and the dark I see me
> it's a halt nothing more I'm journeying it's
> a rest nothing more

It is the condition, too, of Edgar and Caliban – Shakespeare's and Browning's: indeed, Browning's Caliban who

> 'Will sprawl, now that the heat of the day is best,
> Flat on his belly in the pit's much mire,

and who 'talks to his own self' could be Pim: the singing voice is choked by mud, but language does not cease and becomes instead a frantic grunting which has abandoned grammar:

> Pim's then quaqua of us all then mine alone that of us all mine alone after my fashion a murmur in the mud the thin black air nothing left but short waves three hundred four hundred yards per second brief movements of the lower with murmur little tremble flush with the mud one yard two yards me so lively nothing left but words a murmur on and off

It's muddy, this life, this death.

Now to the Churchyard and '*Enter two* CLOWNS', a scene which begins apparently as comic relief but the humour of the clowns consists of their misuse of language: to themselves, there is nothing funny in what they are saying.

It must be *se offendendo*; it cannot be else. For here lies the point: if I drown myself wittingly, it argues an act, and an act hath three branches – it is to act, to do, to perform. Argal, she drowned herself wittingly.

If we substituted the malapropisms with *se defendendo* and *ergo*, the Clown could be a young student at Wittenburg showing off his recently acquired mastery over rhetoric. One has seen people, even educated ones, use language with similar imprecision with the conviction that they had no doubt that they were being precise (and even A. C. Bradley, writing on *Hamlet* in the nineteenth century, could not have had the perspicacity to perceive that he was no better than a clown – and if you wish to extend this example to the present author, of course, I deny being a clown, how dare anyone suggest such a thing, *I* know what I am talking about! And there you perhaps have the truth about this murky business of language: nothing sustains the illusion of logic more than simple human conceit and he who insists on asserting 'I know what I am talking about' is, alas, doubly a clown, being foolish in maintaining he knows anything and being naive in then maintaining that his language is necessarily true).

The dialogue of the clowns is a parody of serious discourse, for their language has the surface appearance of formal correctness but yet is seen by the audience to be laughably absurd: and this absurdity reflects back upon language itself, showing the seemingly logical speech to be ridiculously illogical – cf. Ionesco in *Rhinoceros*:

> LOGICIAN [to the old GENTLEMAN]: Another syllogism. All cats die. Socrates is dead. Therefore Socrates is a cat.

And like both Hamlet and Ophelia who break into verses and songs, the former in the ecstasy of believing he has observed the truth about the King's guilt and the latter in the ecstasy of madness, the Clown, too, breaks into song the substance of which is sexuality and old age, not unlike that of Ophelia's. Truth is again discovered to be the banality of procreation and death but the Clown suffers from no anguish while uttering this truth, spending his life digging grave after grave and having to stand in each grave that he digs without being bothered by the symbolic nature of his action. Hamlet, who has symbolically been sitting on the edge of a grave throughout the play from the moment we see him reflecting upon the unweeded garden, who has seen his father come back from the grave, and who in his 'To be, or not to be' soliloquy has pondered life beyond the grave, now enters the stage to stand physically beside one and says of the skull thrown out by the Clown, 'That skull had a tongue in it, and could sing once.'

Not speak but *sing*, which in the hierarchy of sounds is a superior activity, for speech is condemned to observe responsibility to meaning while song is a self-contained poetical structure of which the idea can be comprehended intuitively. But that song is lost now and the skull reveals nothing: 'Here's fine revolution, an we had the trick to see't.'

The Clown throws out another skull and Hamlet says: 'Why may not that be the skull of a lawyer? Where be his quiddities now, his quillities, his cases, his tenures, and his tricks? Why does he suffer this mad knave now to knock him about the sconce with a dirty shovel, and will not tell him of action of battery? Hum! This fellow might be in's time a great buyer of land, with his statutes, his recognizances, his fines, his double vouchers, his recoveries. Is this the fine of his fines, and the recovery of his recoveries, to have his fine pate full of fine dirt? Will his vouchers vouch him no more of his purchases, and double ones too, than the length and breadth of a pair of indentures? The very conveyances of his lands will scarcely lie in this box, and must th' inheritor himself have no more, ha?'

Why does Hamlet feel compelled to go on and on? The point about the greatest politician or lawyer being reduced to skull and bones is obvious enough to the most naive imagination. It is all those *words* – 'quiddities', 'quillities', etc. – which are exciting Hamlet's brain; the special language of legal contracts which are designed to eliminate, or minimise, the errors of interpretation and to establish certainty of possession is to do with material things, with little patches of ground: the vocabulary of this language is calculated to make definitions precise and to eliminate doubt: what *is* is believed to *be*. The irony which bemuses Hamlet ('They are sheep and calves which seek out assurance in that' he says) is that even so specially structured a language which tries to leave no room for doubt is finally of no help to the people who utter it, and Language is once again seen as merely appearing to be relevant to the human condition.

There follows Hamlet's exchange with the Clown when he asks, 'Whose grave's this, sirrah?' and the Clown answers, 'Mine, sir.' Again, the humour comes from a play on words.

> HAMLET: I think it be thine indeed, for thou liest in't.
> CLOWN: You lie out on't, sir, and therefore 'tis not yours. For my part, I do not lie in't, yet it is mine.

And then:

> HAMLET: What man dost thou dig it for?
> CLOWN: For no man, sir.
> HAMLET: What woman then?
> CLOWN: For none neither.
> HAMLET: Who is to be buried in't?
> CLOWN: One that was a woman, sir; but, rest her soul, she's dead.
> HAMLET: How absolute the knave is! We must speak by the card, or equivocation will undo us.

Although the Clown is seen to be a simpleton, one to whom things must be spelt out to avoid confusion, and therefore a source of humour, he is in fact correct in his speech and that answer, 'One that was a woman, sir; but, rest her soul, she's dead', is as precise as was Hamlet's 'Words, words, words' in answer to Polonius's question about what he was reading.

> HAMLET: How came he mad?
> CLOWN: Very strangely, they say.

HAMLET: How strangely?
CLOWN: Faith, e'en with losing his wits.

Language can only reveal its own rules; a study of language teaches us language-games; it cannot give us an explanation of experience: one is reminded of the example often given by philosophers, 'A husband is a married man'.

Seeing Yorick's skull makes Hamlet utter the gruesome conjuration: 'Now get you to my lady's chamber, and tell her, let her paint an inch thick, to this favour she must come.' Even such wallowing in bitter truth is not sufficient for him. Having observed that politicians and lawyers, creating laws of the land to preserve the form of order, are not themselves preserved, no more than a court jester, Hamlet turns to history, that other illusion of Time and human existence with its vivid imagery of emperors and battles, the greed for patches of ground, a language with its own pretension to incontestable facts:

Alexander died, Alexander was buried, Alexander returneth to dust; the dust is earth; of earth we make loam; and why of that loam whereto he was converted might they not stop a beer barrel?

The great Alexander is reduced to a mere name, a word signifying nothing of history, and the idea of history is mocked by a boyish jingle:

Imperious Caesar, dead and turned to clay,
Might stop a hole to keep the wind away.

Of course, much of the Clown's black humour and Hamlet's easy philosophising perform other functions in the play: Hamlet's return has to be established and the idea suggested that his recent experience at sea, where he has been involved in mortal struggle, has reconciled him to life: his language is now cynical and mocking and not the earlier anguished one demanding answers; the graveside humour and contemplation of skulls is also setting up the scene to effect the greatest dramatic impact and to extract the maximum irony from Ophelia's present burial; but the dialogue has insisted that one note not only the meaning but the idea of Language itself: without the idea of law and history and their relationship with the language on which each is founded, which idea serves as a metaphor for the relationship between reality and language, Hamlet's speeches on seeing the skulls would be trite and serve no purpose than the rather easy one of dramatic irony.

Who is Osric? We have not seen him before and suddenly he appears in the final scene of the play as if he were a long-established courtier. Horatio has not heard of him and Hamlet describes Osric to him in the most contemptuous terms, in an aside:

He hath much land, and fertile. Let a beast be lord of beasts, and his crib shall stand at the king's mess. 'Tis a chough, but, as I say, spacious in the possession of dirt.

The phrase *much land, and fertile* is a contrast with *a little patch of ground* which is barren; and *spacious in the possession of dirt* places Osric firmly among the skulls in the graveyard.

It soon appears that Osric is a dandy, a 'wit' given to florid, euphuistic speech, a lover of superfluous words; he is a caricature of an intelligent human being, the very opposite of Hamlet, impressing his listeners with what he no doubt believes is a refined and an elegant vocabulary but in fact is only a pretentious one; he represents the perversion of an intellectual, for language in his mouth is not a medium of expressing ideas but has become mere decoration, all surface glitter like his clothes and quite empty underneath. The gift of language is reduced to glibness and, as with his hat, Osric cannot put it to its 'right use'. He is a hypocrite, too, agreeing with Hamlet that it is cold and then that it is sultry and hot. When Osric gives a verbose description of Laertes, Hamlet mocks him in his, Osric's, inflated language:

> Sir, his definement suffers no perdition in you, though, I know, to divide him inventorially would dizzy th' arithmetic of memory, and yet but yaw neither in respect of his quick sail. But, in the verity of extolment, I take him to be a soul of great article, and his infusion of such dearth and rareness as, to make true diction of him, his semblable is his mirror, and who else would trace him, his umbrage, nothing more.

In fact, Hamlet out-Osrics Osric in this passage, thus creating a devastating parody of a speech which is already a parody of civilised language. Horatio is bewildered by it and says, 'Is't not possible to understand in another tongue?' Hamlet has taken his verbal revenge, however, and in the process exhausted much of Osric's vocabulary, for Horatio says in an aside to Hamlet: 'His purse is empty already. All's golden words are spent.'

· We reach line 165 of the scene before Osric goes. The message was a simple one: Hamlet is invited to fight a duel with Laertes and that the King has laid a bet on the fight. By contrast to this extravagant scene, soon after Osric has left, a Lord enters with another message from the King, delivers it prosaically within a few lines and exits. The contrast is so deliberately created that one is obliged to look again at Osric and ponder his significance. An extreme decadence of speech (as well as his exaggeratedly foppish appearance) marks him out too conspicuously for him not to be a symbolic representation of so-called civilised man given to a portentous speech which, however, once we examine his seemingly extraordinary combinations of words, is as poor in ideas as it seems rich in vocabulary; and his civilised appearance is only that, an appearance, for he is truly a beast, no more.

We are seeing, too, in the figure of Osric, what Hamlet might easily have become, a popular, 'witty' courtier charming everyone with his pretty speeches, one who never questions the emptiness of his trendy words. Osric's language emphasises the idea of the failure of language, and Hamlet, bitterly mocking Osric, is spitting out a frenzy of worthless words, because he has very nearly reached a point where he must reject language and embrace silence.

A mood of resignation seems to have come over Hamlet, though his mind continues to play with verbal formulae – 'If it be now, 'tis not to come; if it be not to come, it will be now; if it be not now, yet it will come.' (Cf. Beckett in *Watt*: 'For what is this shadow of the going in which we come, this shadow of the coming in which we go, this shadow of the coming and the going in which we wait, if not the shadow of purpose, of the purpose that budding withers, that withering buds, whose blooming is a budding withering? I speak well, do I not, for a man in my situation?') To this juggling of words, Hamlet adds, 'Let be.' These two words are spoken softly, as if he were dismissing all propositions out of his mind, and are possibly drowned by the trumpets and drums which announce the arrival of the King, the Queen and 'all the State', and one is distracted from noticing that that 'Let be' is Hamlet's final statement before the dramatic events of the last scene and that 'Let be' is, of course, the resolution in his mind of that debate in which 'To be, or not to be' was one proposition of which to test the implications. Now he realises that life

offers no alternative but to let be, for the events will over-
take us, absorbing us in their riotous unpredictability: no
amount of contemplation and the probing of language will
stifle the loud trumpets which replace the ideas of life with
a pageant of the living. But even in his resolution to accept
action, Hamlet is driven by the habits of his mind, and
asking Laertes to pardon him, says:

> Was't Hamlet wronged Laertes? Never Hamlet.
> If Hamlet from himself be ta'en away,
> And when he's not himself does wrong Laertes,
> Then Hamlet does it not, Hamlet denies it.
> Who does it then? His madness. If't be so,
> Hamlet is of the faction that is wronged;
> His madness is poor Hamlet's enemy.

It is a passage in which he has reduced his own behaviour
to a verbal formula, making his own name into an object
(just as he had earlier with 'Alexander').

They prepare to play and the King ceremoniously makes
a grandiose speech – 'Set me the stoups of wine upon the
table.'

> And let the kettle to the trumpet speak,
> The trumpet to the cannoneer without,
> The cannons to the heavens, the heaven to earth . . .

The trumpet speak. And let there be such a thunderous
noise that his own lies are drowned in a violent elimination
of silence, that state in which humans are liable to ponder
meanings or to which they are reduced when all attempts
at meaning have been exhausted. But the King loses in
this final attempt to camouflage his own evil intention, and
the sounds which command attention when the King, the

Queen and Laertes are lying dead on the stage are the
words of Hamlet's dying voice:

> O, I could tell you –
> But let it be.

There is more anguish in that *could tell* than is due to the
frustration of not having time to explain himself, and he
asks Horatio to 'tell my story': he himself cannot explain
himself and sinks into a final silence.

Fortinbras, whose business in this world has been like
Alexander's, to go about conquering a little patch of
ground, enters a moment after Hamlet dies and this is the
first time we see him at the court in Elsinore. Four mem-
bers of Denmark's nobility lie dead before him in a vivid
metaphor, reducing the court to another worthless little
patch of ground, for death is the principal reality visible
on it, but Fortinbras is not one given to perceiving ironies
or even meaning, for he sees this devastation as his 'fortune'
– 'For me, with sorrow I embrace my fortune.' Before
doing so, he makes a token gesture in a rhetorical
language:

> O proud Death,
> What feast is toward in thine eternal cell
> That thou so many princes at a shot
> So bloodily hast struck?

His mind comprehends only the imagery of action and he
inflicts upon the dead Hamlet the role of a soldier which
he never was in life:

> Let four captains
> Bear Hamlet like a soldier to the stage . . .

and as if this is not sufficient irony, Fortinbras unwittingly gives us more:

> and for his passage
> The soldiers' music and the rite of war
> Speak loudly for him.

Speak loudly. But no longer in words.

*   *   *

And in *Waiting for Godot*:

ESTRAGON: In the meantime let us try and converse calmly, since we are incapable of keeping silent.

. . .

VLADIMIR: Say something!
ESTRAGON: I'm trying.

Long silence.